YOUTH WITHOUT REPRESENTATION

YOUTH WITHOUT REPRESENTATION

The Absence of Young Adults in Parliaments, Cabinets, and Candidacies

Daniel Stockemer and Aksel Sundström

UNIVERSITY OF MICHIGAN PRESS

ANN ARBOR

Published in the United States of America by the
University of Michigan Press
Manufactured in the United States of America
Printed on acid-free paper
First published December 2022

A CIP catalog record for this book is available from the British Library.

Library of Congress Cataloging-in-Publication data has been applied for.

ISBN 978-0-472-07517-1 (hardcover : alk. paper)
ISBN 978-0-472-05517-3 (paper : alk. paper)
ISBN 978-0-472-90284-2 (open access ebook)

https://doi.org/10.3998/mpub.11459940

An electronic version of this book is freely available, thanks to the support of libraries working with Knowledge Unlatched (KU). KU is a collaborative initiative designed to make high quality books Open Access for the public good. More information about the initiative and links to the Open Access version can be found at www.knowledgeunlatched.org

The University of Michigan Press's open access publishing program is made possible thanks to additional funding from the University of Michigan Office of the Provost and the generous support of contributing libraries.

Contents

Digital materials related to this title can be found on the Fulcrum platform
via the following citable URL https://doi.org/10.3998/mpub.11459940

List of Figures

List of Tables

Acknowledgments

The authors acknowledge generous support from the Konrad Adenauer Stiftung Canada Office, the Social Science and Humanities Research Council of Canada, and the Swedish Research Council.

CHAPTER 1

INTRODUCTION

> I think the old age of legislators is a problem. We have the world's largest
> generation ever of adolescents and youth. So if decisions are being made
> by an age cohort that is decades above that and is not attuned to their
> perspective I think it's a serious democratic deficit. I used to be of the view
> that people needed to come in to parliaments with some degree of maturity
> and background. I actually no longer think that. I think a parliament is a
> place where young people with fresh perspectives should be. And I think
> our political system should accommodate that.
>
> (HELEN CLARK, FORMER NEW ZEALAND PRIME MINISTER,
> INTERVIEW WITH THE AUTHORS)

The political elite in most countries is conceived mainly of wealthy, educated, and senior men of the dominant ethnicity. National parliaments and cabinets are arenas that fit this description: they "include more of the affluent than the less well-off, more men than women, more middle-aged than young, and more white-collar professionals than blue-collar workers" (Norris 1997, 6). In particular, young citizens are an "excluded majority" (IPU 2014), with an insufficient presence. People under the age of 35 represent more than half of today's world population, but in political office, whether elected or appointed, youth are a clear minority. For example, our own calculations of a global sample of national parliaments show that young people aged 18 to 35 years are not even represented at a ratio of one to three when we compare their presence in parliament with their share of the general population. In cabinets, this ratio is even less favorable for youth, nearly one to ten. We argue in this book that this discrepancy is a democratic deficit.

The United States of America (U.S.) is the prime, but certainly not the only, example of a polity with senior leaders, where the political class is not representative of the population. At the end of 2021, some of the most important politicians are beyond 65 years of age. The president, Joe Biden, is 79 years old; the Senate majority leader, Chuck Schumer, is 71 years; the Senate minority leader, Mitch McConnell, is 79 years old; and the speaker of the House of Representatives, Nancy Pelosi, is 80 years old. In November 2020, Americans had the choice between two presidential candidates in their 70s, the incumbent Donald Trump and his challenger Joe Biden. Given that Biden's toughest primary contender, Bernie Sanders, was also in his late 70s, the magazine *The Atlantic* described the presidential race in March 2020 as follows: "We have now before us three candidates divided by ideology, but united in dotage. All three white men were born in the 1940s, before the invention of Velcro and the independence of India and Israel. Amazingly, each is currently older than any of the past three U.S. presidents."[1] The seniority of politicians goes beyond the figureheads of the two main parties. The 117th Congress of the United States (January 2021 to January 2023) is one of the oldest to have ever served. The average American was about 20 years younger than the average representative in the United States' lower house, who was 58 years old at the time of the swearing-in of Congress in early 2021.

Yet the old age of politicians is not only a feature of the United States. Rather, several of the largest democracies are real gerontocracies, political systems in which older people have better chances of attaining leadership positions and are largely overrepresented in such seats (Magni-Berton and Panel 2021). In India, for example, the world's most populated democracy, the median age of the population is 28 years old. However, the median age of members in the lower house of the Indian Parliament, the Lok Sabha, and the cabinet was almost 57 years as of 2021.[2] Japan is another "silver democracy" (referring to the dominant hair color in the Japanese Diet), considering that youth are literally absent in this elected assembly (see Sota 2018). The day of the constitution of the parliament in 2017, young parliamentarians 35 years or under made up only 2.6 percent of the legislature, and parliamentarians 40 years or under 7.8 percent. In Prime Minister Abe's cabinet, there was not a single minister aged 40 or under at the time of its formation in 2017.

In several countries in less economically developed parts of the world, including Namibia and Angola, the gap in the age distribution between members of parliament (MPs) and citizens is even larger. In Namibia, for example, the median age of the population was around 21 years old in 2019, while the median age of MPs was 59 years old. On average, cabinet members in this African country were 2.5 years older than their counterparts in parliament. In Angola, the gap is even more pronounced. The median age

---

1. Thomson, D. "Why Do Such Elderly People Run America? Sanders is too old. So is Biden. Trump too." *The Atlantic*, March 5, 2020. https://www.theatlantic.com/ideas/archive/2020/03/why-are-these-people-so-freaking-old/607492/

2. See http://164.100.47.194/Loksabha/Members/MemberSearchByAge.aspx

among citizens was 16 years in 2015; as such, the majority of the population did not have the right to vote. In contrast, the median age of parliamentarians in 2015 was 63.5 years. Cabinet members were slightly younger (i.e., the median and mean age was both 61.5 years). Nevertheless, this leaves us with a stunning age difference of 45 years between the median age in the population and the median age of their appointed leaders.

The stylized figure below (fig. 1) illustrates the visible absence of young adults in parliaments. The size of each horizontal block displays the number of people in a certain age category in a setting that mimics the average country today (roughly based on our parliamentary dataset). By visualizing the numerical distribution across age cohorts, the figure illustrates that there is a clear discrepancy in the ratio between young adults in the population and young adults in office. In many countries, they are often the largest cohort in the population of eligible voters yet the smallest one in the legislature in terms of their descriptive presence. If we were to draw the same figure for cabinets, the age distribution would be even more detrimental for young adults as ministers.

In this book, we focus on the marginalization of young adults in politics, taking a comparative focus on legislatures, cabinets, and candidacies for office. Normatively, our starting point is that a democracy or any system of government cannot flourish if it systematically excludes one cohort of the adult population. In the words of Scharpf (1999, 6), "[p]olitical choices are legitimate if they reflect the 'will of the people'—that is, if they can be derived from the authentic preferences of the members of a community." We deduct from this statement that young adults ought to be present in assemblies to a larger extent than they are contemporarily. Theoretically, we embed youths' lack of political representation within a framework, which we label the *vicious cycle of political alienation*, between declining political interest of the young, their lack of conventional political participation, and their inadequate representation in political office. Empirically, we display the magnitude of this underrepresentation and explain variation in the presence of youth as candidates for elected office, in parliaments and in cabinets around the world. To fulfill this goal, we use novel data both cross-nationally and over time to investigate the representation of young adults within the candidate pool, in parliaments and cabinets across the greatest number of countries and times possible. The argument we make has relevance for settings across the world, and the empirical data we analyze is global, coupled with insights from settings where data availability, or contrasting cases, allow us to make in-depth inferences.

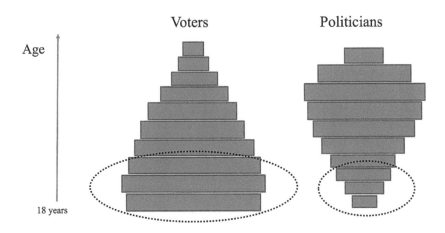

Figure 1. The age distribution in parliaments and the age distribution among voters

To provide this holistic account of youth representation in the legislative branch, across parties' parliamentary delegations, as candidates and in the executive, we present six chapters—one theoretical chapter and five empirical ones.

In chapter 2, we situate our study within the broader literature on youth participation and youth representation. We start by defining youth as a concept and illustrate why youth representation matters. Mainly building on Mansbridge (1999, 2005), we make a normative argument for why young adults ought to have a larger descriptive political presence. At the heart of this chapter is what we label a vicious cycle of political alienation between declining political sophistication of the young, their waning (conventional) political participation, and their insufficient representation in political office. We explain that because of societal tendencies, including changes in political socialization, a lack of civic education in school, and maturation at a later age (just to name a few factors), young citizens are less and less interested in conventional politics and participate less and less in the political process. This political apathy then renders the voice of young adults less important because parties and candidates gain relatively little from catering to the interests of a group that largely refrains from voting. This also applies to the nomination of candidates: since youth tend to abstain from voting more than the middle-aged or elderly, there is less of an incentive for parties to nominate younger candidates. Completing this vicious cycle, we illustrate that if we do not change course, we can expect young adults to become even more indifferent to the representative system as they realize that the larger political system neglects their agenda and that candidates bear little resemblance to themselves. We end the chapter by showing that one way to break this vicious cycle is to increase young individuals' political representation. Granting the young adequate representation could allow younger cohorts to bring their topics of importance to the political agenda, which in turn could entice young adults to participate in the political process.

Chapter 3 focuses on youth representation in parliament. First, we examine the current state of age representation in more than 120 parliaments and find that young adults aged 35 years or under make up less than 10 percent of the parliamentarians at the onset of each parliament and around 20 percent of MPs aged 40 years or under. Second, we retrace youth representation in four national parliaments (Australia, France, Germany, and the United Kingdom) over several decades and report no improvement over time in the presence of youth in parliament. Third, we conduct an aggregate-level analysis on the national level, illustrating why some legislatures have younger representatives than others. As explanatory factors, we focus on national-level covariates, including institutional variables (e.g., the existence of youth quotas, the electoral system type, and candidate age requirements) and socioeconomic indicators (e.g., share of Muslims in the population, level of corruption, level of development, and the median age of the population). Our models highlight the importance of two explanatory factors: 1) lower age requirements to stand for candidacy matter, in that they make parliaments younger and increase the presence of politicians aged 35 or 40 years or under; 2) proportional representation (PR) systems trigger an increase in the share of young politicians (but PR systems do not make the parliament younger overall). We conclude this chapter with a discussion of youth quotas, highlighting the potential that such rules of affirmative action could have if applied more forcefully.

In chapter 4, we switch the analysis from the national level to the meso- or party level and study party delegations. Focusing on more than 250 parties in 52 countries, we confirm the underrepresentation of youth in parties' groups across the restrictive sample of delegations. Graphing youth representation of the delegations from the major parties in our four respective countries, we also validate the finding that youth representation has not increased over the past decades. However, what we find is that there is more variation in the age representation of party delegations in legislatures than there is variation across parliaments. Our multivariate analyses explain this variation by mainly two factors: the age of political parties and the age of party leaders. Our results illustrate that young parties generally have younger MPs, but as these parties mature representatives get older as well. In addition, younger party leaders trigger a young(er) legislative party group. Similar to the chapter on parliaments, we end this chapter with a discussion of the potential influence of party quotas, as a fast-track mechanism to correct the imbalance in youth representation in politics vis-à-vis the adult population as a whole.

In chapter 5, we leave the parliamentary arena and focus on cabinets. Even more so than in parliaments, we find that youth in cabinets are extremely rare: young adults do not even have a third of the representation they have in parliaments. Similar to legislatures, we also find that youth representation in the cabinets we study across time has not increased over the past decades. While young adults are generally scarce in cabinets across the globe, there are notable differences between countries. Some cabinets, such as the current one in New Zealand, has about 20 percent young ministers and the average age among ministers is below 50 years. In other countries, such as India or China, the average minister is presently above 60 years and rarely is a single cabinet member below the age of 40. What explains this variation? Focusing on attributes of the nominator such as their age, as well as national level factors such as the size of the cabinet and youth representation in parliament, we find two factors to be important. First, on average, young leaders nominate younger cabinet members. Second, the number of young MPs in the national parliament appears crucial for the selection of young ministers. We conclude the chapter with an analysis of the portfolios young ministers occupy. Distinguishing between high-prestige, medium-prestige, and low-prestige portfolios, we find that the age of ministers in high-prestige portfolios is higher than the age of ministers in medium- or low-prestige portfolios, and that there are fewer young ministers on high-prestige positions.

We complement the macro- and meso-level analyses in chapters 3 to 5 with some more individual-level analyses in the two final empirical chapters of the book. In chapter 6, we use the Comparative Candidate Study (CCS) dataset, which covers 18 elections in 14 countries, to compare young candidates with young representatives. The first finding from this analysis is that there are plenty of young candidates; in fact, young candidates aged 35 years or under make up nearly 30 percent of all contenders in our sample of 18 elections. Young candidates aged 40 years or under constitute more than 40 percent of all candidates. We also highlight that most of these young candidates have high party capital: they are as strongly engaged in their parties as their more senior colleagues. However, what is missing among young candidates is electoral capital: they tend to lack the contacts and resources necessary to gain nomination for a winnable district in a majoritarian system, or an eligible list position in a proportional system. In addition, and using the example of Switzerland, we provide preliminary evidence for this gap between young candidates and young elected representatives. Parties use youth as "fillers"—that is, they place them on list positions that in practice have little chances of winning, or on special youth lists that normally do not elect anybody to the national parliament. In addition, it also seems that voters tend to vote for candidates in the older age groups.

The final empirical section of the book, chapter 7, provides insights from two settings: Sweden and Switzerland. Sweden represents a case where young adults have relatively high representation in the national parliament and where young candidates have a high chance of being elected. Switzerland represents a case where the system has not yet managed to accommodate calls for having more young adults in politics and where young candidates, despite being high in numbers, have a low chance of being elected. Having sent out a survey to both representatives and candidates in these two settings, the chapter seeks to understand how age is politicized, the extent to which survey respondents perceive age discrimination, and what factors seem to explain the contrasting outcomes in the two countries. We also wanted to know from MPs and candidates which factors they think could help increase youths' representation. Briefly, we mainly explain Sweden's comparatively high levels of youth representation by a somewhat youth friendly political culture. This relative youth friendliness takes the shape of implicit or explicit arrangements to represent the population as closely as possible on party lists and strong youth wings that successfully lobby for the nomination of young candidates. In contrast, while MPs and candidates in Switzerland note that youth have a low presence, there seems to be a reluctance of admitting that such patterns are an outcome of age discrimination. The survey responses from both countries further hint that both political cultures strongly value "experience" as a trait among politicians, albeit at different degrees. This strong emphasis of experience is frequently detrimental for the presence of young politicians. Several of our survey participants further highlight that belittling and derogatory attitudes toward youth are still quite widespread in the national parliaments and other political assemblies in the two countries.

Chapter 8 concludes the book. We summarize our main findings and then provide some recommendations of what political elites, individual MPs and candidates, and voters can do to make politics more inclusive for young adults. Specifically, we highlight what we see as constructive reforms that could increase the political representation of young adults. Among others, we recommend the abolishment of age barriers for young adults to stand for political office, term limits for a seat in the national assembly, and the selection of a young party leader.

CHAPTER 2

WHY WE NEED INCREASED YOUTH REPRESENTATION

The world needs to move beyond platitudes about young people. We need meaningful opportunities for youth engagement in government systems and in the democratic process.

(ANTÓNIO GUTERRES, UN SECRETARY-GENERAL)

2.1. Youth: An Important Group of Study

Age is a fluid concept that has both an objective and a subjective meaning. As Hainz (2015) notes, "there is no objective threshold that separates young people from people who are not young any more" (24). Age is also somewhat of a malleable concept in the sense that being of a certain age could have a different meaning across various settings and in different times. For example, being 30 is already quite old in some settings with low life expectancy, such as Afghanistan or Zimbabwe. In other settings with life expectancies of 80 years or more, 30 years of age is still young. Individuals are also in different stages of life at the same age in different parts of the world. In Western countries such as Canada, Germany, or Switzerland many individuals are unmarried and do not have children in their early 30s. In contrast, on the African continent most women marry just after the age of 20 years and even earlier than the age of 18 in some settings, which is a pervasive pattern in countries such as Niger and Nigeria (UNICEF 2018).

In addition to being a fluid concept, age is also a temporary state in somebody's life. Most group features are rather stable for an individual (e.g., gender identity or religious minority status seldom changes for an individual over time) and rest on well-identifiable markers (such as having a uterus—for most individuals identifying as women—or making a confession to a certain religion). However, belonging to the group of young people is different from belonging to other politically marginalized groups. Ageing is inevitable for every person and being young is thus not a permanent feature. For that reason, we could ask the question: should we be paying attention to a group with whom a majority of individuals will only have a

9

temporary identification? Our answer is yes. Adolescents and young adults up to the age of 30 or 35 become aware of what happens around them; they develop their political values, political ambition, and political habits during these formative years (Jennings and Stoker 2004). They become children of their time with shared attributes and associations (see Munger 2021); each generation develops its own defining features, which show a clear connection with some shared views about politics and society.

But how do we define youth? Only focusing on whether or not people identify as young adults would not be very useful for us given that somebody who is 60 years of age could in theory self-identify as young.[1] Instead when we use the term "youth" as a group, we try to refer to the attribute of being in a certain objective age category, rather than the self-identification as young. We believe that the number of years a person has lived should be an unproblematic way of measuring age for most people. We use this age-based approach partly because of pragmatism and partly because research on young adults in politics generally uses this approach. Also for our empirical analyses we cannot leave the definition of youth open and rely on individuals' self-identification (see Barrett and Pachi 2019). Rather, to determine the level of youth underrepresentation, we need a clear definition including a lower and upper age limit.[2]

While an array of influential bodies—ranging from UNICEF and other UN agencies to the African Youth Charter and the Council of Europe—debate the exact age span that youth refers to, we assume that a lower bar of 18 years is a reasonable delimitation for how to define young adults. In most countries we study, 18 is the lower bar of age of majority, the threshold in which the law recognizes adulthood (which most frequently comes with the right to vote and sometimes the right to stand for office).[3] For the upper limit, definitions range from 35 to 45 years (see IPU 2014, 2016, 2018, 2021). To capture this range, we set two upper age limits throughout this book: 35 and 40 years old. When studying candidates, legislators, and cab-

---

1. To underline that age is a clearly defined feature, we can point to a legal case of a 69-year-old Dutchman, who wanted to change his legal age, arguing that age is a social construction. The courts denied this petition (BBC 2018).

2. Another illustration of how current debates politicize age are claims favoring the expansion of the franchise to children (e.g., giving the children's parents the right to cast an additional vote for each child they have) (see Chen and Clayton [2006] and *The Economist* [2017] for a discussion of such propositions).

3. We should note that some settings, such as Austria, as well as numerous settings at the local level across the world, have experimented with letting 16-year-olds participate in elections (see Wagner et al. 2014; Eichhorn and Bergh 2020).

inet members we focus on the age at the time of candidacy, the election, or the nomination. These two upper limits capture the current definitions of youth in politics. To illustrate, somebody who wins election at the age of 40 will normally terminate her term in elected office at the age of 45 at the latest. In the empirical analyses, we also present the median and mean age of the candidate pool in parliaments, in parliamentary party delegations, and in cabinets to have an overall idea of the age distribution in these entities.

2.2. The Importance of Group Representation for Youth

We believe that group representation matters. Conover (1988) made this point very clear more than 30 years ago, when she wrote:

> [t]he way we think about social groups depends enormously on whether we are part of that group. Try as we might, the political sympathy that we feel for other groups is never quite the same as that which these groups feel for themselves or that which we feel for ourselves (75).

A large strand of the literature on the link between descriptive and substantive representation concurs with this claim. To clarify how descriptive representation differs from substantive representation, Pitkin (1972, 209) defines the substantive ideal as one where an elected representative "acting in the interest of the represented, in a manner responsive to them." Following this distinction, Mansbridge (1999, 629) outlines how the descriptive presence of groups rests on the idea that "representatives are in their own persons and lives in some sense typical of the larger class of persons whom they represent." This normative argument in favor of social group representation suggests that representatives of a specific group take into consideration their constituents' groups' wishes when making decisions. In particular, if a parliament has none or very few members of a certain group, this assembly might face problems of upholding legitimacy over its decision among voters that strongly identify with this group (Norris and Franklin 1997). Of course, empirically there is no guarantee that representatives either share such a relation of identity or similarity with constituents or act in the interest of these constituencies (see Wood and Young 1997). The literature nevertheless suggests that the legislative presence of certain underrepresented groups is potentially important (see Phillips 1995, 1998).

But what groups deserve representation? The challenge, Young (1989) notes, is the following: "The principle of group representation calls for structures of representation for oppressed or disadvantaged groups" (265). This begs the question: what groups can we consider as being disadvantaged? For obvious reasons, most would agree that left-handers or redheads do not meet conditions for deserving political representation. Therefore "mirror views provide few guidelines for selecting which social characteristics merit representation" (Morone and Marmor 1981, 437). Nevertheless, Kymlicka (1995) identifies two contextual arguments that can justify forms of group representation under certain circumstances, one being when groups demand self-government and the other being when group representation is a means to overcome systemic disadvantage (144). The first criterion mainly applies to ethnic or religious groups and for territorial representation. Yet we do not see this aspect as very relevant for young people.

What about the second criterion—do youth face systematic disadvantage? At first glance, age is not necessarily a factor with which we should be particularly concerned. If women and ethnic minorities do not gain representation in parliaments, they will potentially face unequal treatment in comparison with other citizens throughout their whole life. In contrast, if young people do not gain descriptive representation, they will not face unequal treatment over their complete lives, if compared with individuals from other age groups who were young themselves at some point in time. According to this life-cycle argument, the exclusion of young adults in decision-making bodies is less unfair than the absence of women (see Phillips 1998, 229). Based on such observations, we could conclude that "a society that heavily discriminates between people on grounds of age can still treat people equally, if we consider their access to given resources over their complete lives. Everyone's turn will come" (Gosseries 2007 quoted in Bidadanure 2015a). However, at second glance, we deem such a conclusion highly premature and argue that young adults ought to have a voice in elected assemblies and in nominations through their descriptive presence.

The literature acknowledges that focusing on descriptive representation of groups might come at the expense of other democratic principles. It could give rise to costs when voters potentially start focusing on the characteristics of legislators, rather than on the decisions and policies in focus. Mansbridge argues that one evident cost is "that of strengthening tendencies toward 'essentialism,' that is, the assumption that members of certain groups have an essential identity that all members of that group share and of which no others can partake" (1999, 637). Other authors acknowledge that institutionalizing group differences through their political presence could have serious implications for social unity (Kymlicka 1995). Voicing the need for one group's claim for descriptive presence also has implications: it could assume that people from this group cannot adequately represent others (Phillips 1995). Given the possible risk of these essentializing features that come with group representation, we want to explicitly make the case for why young adults should gain increased representation. To do so, we build on Mansbridge's (1999, 2015) framework, which discusses the conditions under which we should accept the costs of descriptive representation. According to her, the presence in legislatures for a certain group becomes particularly important to the democratic process in five distinct contexts, which are: 1) uncrystallized substantive interests, 2) a social understanding of the group as "unfit to rule," 3) diminished legitimacy of governmental decisions, 4) a history of communicative mistrust, and 5) failures elsewhere in the system of representation. In our opinion, all five contexts apply to varying degrees to youth underrepresentation.

2.2.1. Five Criteria for Why Young Adults Need Descriptive Representation

Uncrystallized Substantive Interests

As Mansbridge (1999, 648) notes, "disadvantaged groups may need descriptive representation in order to get un-crystallized substantive interests represented with sufficient vigor." So what are these so-called uncrystallized substantive interests? Mansbridge mentions three conditions. The first is the existence of goals, values, and policy preferences of the out-group in question that differ significantly of those of the in-group (which have various advantages). The second condition is that the political system—including the government, parties, and the media system—does not fully articulate these views and preferences. This latter point also implies that other existing political cleavages in society are unable to capture these differences. The third condition is that there are policies that affect the out-group differently from the in-group.

The first condition of different interests applies to young adults. In particular, in Western countries, young adults in countries such as the United States develop a political identity through cohort consciousness among Millennials and Generation Z (see Munger 2021). One characteristic of such cohort consciousness is that young individuals share some overarching values. For example, younger individuals, such as those belonging to Gen Z, tend to have more pluralistic, multicultural, and egalitarian beliefs, whereas older individuals have a tendency to hold rather traditional attitudes (Abramson and Inglehart 2009). For example, using the American National Election Survey, Wattenberg (2015) shows how older generations in the United States tend to be more likely to identify as a conservative, favor large spending on the military, and are more likely to reject policies to reduce income inequalities. In contrast, younger individuals, in the majority, identify as progressive, left leaning, and favor public spending for health care, education, and social services. When it comes to societal questions, McEvoy (2016) further highlights that opinions among Europeans to same-sex marriage vary significantly based on age, with younger citizens being more open and supportive toward this possibility and older citizens more opposed to it (see also Sevi 2021). In some important referendums, such as the 2016 vote on Brexit, it seems that age was a clear dividing line: compared to older voters, young voters were much more likely to be in support of the "remain" camp (i.e., they favored that the United Kingdom remains within the European Union) (Sloam 2016; Phillips et al. 2018). In addition, some specific policy proposals have contrasting appeal among older cohorts compared to younger ones (Curry and Haydon 2018; Bailer et al. 2022). For example, a policy proposal geared at reducing tuition costs is much more likely to energize youth than it is to energize older individuals.

Second, it seems that "a significant aspect of the political bias in favor of the elderly involves the issues that make it to the political agenda" (Wattenberg 2015, 156). A case in point is the one of climate change. Compared to older citizens, young citizens are more concerned about anthropogenic emissions of greenhouse gases and believe that the problem is a top political issue. For instance, a 2018 Gallup Poll shows that young U.S. citizens have a higher likelihood to label global warming a problem compared to older ones. According to Gallup "70% of Americans aged 18 to 34 worry about global warming. This compares with 62% of those 35 to 54 [years] and 56% who are 55 or older." Older politicians have also frequently brushed aside the urgency of global warming. The prime example is former president Donald Trump, who during his tenure not only removed the United States from the Paris Climate Agreement but also repeatedly called global warming a "hoax" (Time 2019).

The school strikes, which rose in the spring of 2019 throughout the world to protect the climate (known variously as Fridays for Future protests, or Youth for Climate protest) (see New York Times 2019) exemplify the generational dimension of the environment issue. Activists from the young generation have articulated that the old generation left the pollution to be cleaned up by them. Because many governments have closed formal channels to voice this injustice and demand action, the young generation is more and more willing to resort to unconventional means and engage in protest and street demonstrations. Given the strong concerns of most young people about climate change, it is likely that if a larger share of young adults were in power, such politicians would take more action to address this challenge (for a discussion of this possibility, see Karnein and Roser 2015).[4]

The example of the climate also highlights the generational contrast in how policies could affect different age cohorts. Compared to older people, young adults have a greater stake in defining how the future might look (see Van Parijs 1998; Flanagan 2016). There are plenty of other issues where the policies of those in power (i.e., older politicians) might not align with the overall wishes of those of younger cohorts. This might be especially true for spending priorities of public funds, where the interest of younger generations might stand in contrast to those of the older ones. For example, empirical findings suggest that young adults tend to favor free secondary and tertiary education, while the middle-aged may be more averse to increased taxation and the elderly might prefer higher pensions (see Furlong and Cartmel 2012; Sorensen 2013; Jennings and Niemi 2014).[5]

Historically Seen as "Unfit to Rule"

Historically, societies have repeatedly made judgment of who can govern. Mansbridge (1999) notes that there is often a social construction related to a group's ability to rule: "In certain historical conditions, what it means to be a member of a particular social group includes some form of 'second-class citizenship'" (648). Traditionally, groups considered unfit to rule included women, less wealthy citizens, ethnic and religious minorities, and the young. The history of humankind is full of normative and empirical justifications of why young adults are not *regierungsfähig*—or not suitable or experienced enough to stand for office. For instance, Plato believed that individuals reached philosophical maturity after the age of 50 years (see McKee and Barber 2001). Such notions of age-related suitability have translated into unspoken as well as outright formalized rules determining which adults have the right to govern. Age barriers to stand for elections have a

---

4. Empirically, it seems also true that climate change is a priority of some young head of governments. Examples are Emmanuel Macron or Justin Trudeau. See also our empirical analysis later in this chapter.

5. See Sorensen (2013) for a nuanced discussion on cohort-effects, generation-effects, and period-effects on support for different types of public spending.

long tradition. For example, *lex Villia Annalis* (180 years BC) regulated the "the ages at which one could seek and hold each magistracy" in the Roman Empire more than 2,000 years ago (Rögler 1962).[6] Today we see similar rules in over 40 countries, including settings as different as Japan, Nigeria, and Tajikistan. To take these examples, the minimum age to run for national office in Japan is 25 years; in Nigeria it is 30; and in Tajikistan it is 35. In other countries, such as the United States, there are still numerous rules related to somebody's age that hinder young adults to participate fully as democratic citizens (Seery 2011). For example, the 26th Amendment lowered the voting age in 1971 from 21 to 18 years, but it did not fully alter rules regarding the right to stand for office. To illustrate, to be a senator, a person must be at least 30. To be a representative, a person must be at least 25 years old.[7] Kamikubo (2019) argues that such rules tend to exclude students (often under the age of 25 years) from running for office, and as such they might effectively end graduates' nascent involvement in formal politics, which was ignited through student politics.

Even in other settings, with no formal age barriers, "'political experience' is frequently one of the main criteria for judging the 'quality' of elected officials" (Krook and Nugent 2018, 62; see also Weeks and Baldez 2015). Clearly, if suitability for office were an aggregation of experience from prior assignments, then only the very oldest candidates would be suitable for office. Yet we believe that this principle of experience should not be the only guiding principle for who our elected and selected representatives should be. Of course, it is possibly true that a politician with decades of experience could have the network and connections within the elite of a country, as well as the expertise to conduct difficult negotiations. Nevertheless, we think that in addition to these potential merits of a more "technocratic" view on suitability for office—which primarily values expert knowledge—citizens also ask for representatives that innovate and bring new topics to the table (Celis and Childs 2008). After all, calls for political change and demands for reform might very well require rejuvenation of the ranks of representatives and recruitment of people that have not been a part of the system for long.

---

6. The original transcript read, "quot annos nati quemque magistratum peterent caperentque" (Townshend 2017).

7. The bar of the voting age at 21 in the United States seems to be a historical remnant, borrowed from a tradition in the British common law. Supposedly, the practice stems from medieval ages, as 21 "was the age at which a medieval adolescent was thought capable of wearing a suit of heavy armor and was therefore eligible for knighthood" (Cheng 2016, 9, cited in Douglas 2020).

Yet the reality in many countries is that political candidates benefit from their "political experience," as accumulated merit is often a strong—or the only—criterion for nomination (Magni-Berton and Panel 2021). Seasoned players tend to have better connections within the party as well. For example, those within the in-group of political parties (i.e., other senior party officials) will receive an advantage in running for office through their network, since they are part of a group that outsiders have difficulty penetrating. In addition, closed networks have an increased need for trust and an inherent motivation to relate to other members of the network, who may not break this trust (Bjarnegård 2013). This might create an inherent bias against the nomination of newcomers such as young politicians. In addition, in situations with a strong network structure, actors in these elite circles may take an instrumental approach and expect (new) members to bring social, financial, and political resources—something young people are unlikely to have (Bjarnegård 2018).

The expectation of experience and seniority as prime criteria for candidate selection not only discriminates on the individual level but also leads to the homogenization of legislatures and cabinets (i.e., senior men of the dominant ethnic group occupy the majority of political offices). Pejoratively, we can label most parliaments and cabinets as "old boys' clubs" (see McDonald 2011). However, having a very uniform assembly of older members goes counter to ideals of diversity and inclusion. These homogenous parliaments are also suboptimal from a policy perspective. Countries with stagnated representatives do not move forward and modernize their status-quo politics; they are unlikely to thrive with new ideas, innovation, and political renewal. We believe that young politicians are more likely to push new issues to the agenda than older ones.[8] Bidadanure (2015a, 2021) points out further that gerontocracy has many undesirable properties, not the least of which being that it lowers the ability to achieve intergenerational justice, which is arguably salient when future generations are at risk from today's decisions (see also Magni-Berton and Panel 2021). For example, young leaders are likely to have a different stand in a range of issues, which not only includes global warming but also issues like gender equality or same-sex marriage. In these areas, younger politicians could bring much-needed change (see discussion in Sevi 2021). In particular, with ever-increasing levels of education for each generation,

---

8. This is related to recent work by Munger (2021), who speaks about the "boomer ballast" in the United States, where the baby boomer generation is indeed a political force that contributes to making societal change slower.

we also believe that young politicians are likely to have enough skills and knowledge to become excellent representatives and cabinet members. Therefore the dominance of the elderly in legislatures cannot be justified based on their "natural superiority of talent" anymore (Phillips 1995, 65).

Diminished Legitimacy of Government Decisions

The descriptive absence of certain groups in the national legislature and other elected bodies risks undermining the legitimacy of the political system in the eyes of those without representation (Norris and Franklin 1997). A prime example of such illegitimacy would be the centuries of discrimination against Black people in the United States. Up to the present time, their historical underrepresentation in formal politics has weakened the legitimacy they perceive toward government. Is the absence of youth in legislatures causing young citizens to see governments as illegitimate? This question is certainly difficult to answer, but there are obvious signs that many youth are appalled by the political system. For example, using the example of U.S. politics, the study by Lawless and Fox (2015) provides plenty of examples of youth feeling disconnected with the system. This sentiment connects with a low willingness among young Americans to engage in conventional politics. They summarize youths' disgust with the system as follows:

> Washington's dreadful performance over the past two decades has taken a toll on the young Americans who have come to know politics through this spectacle. They see politics as pointless and unpleasant. They see political leaders as corrupt and selfish (8).

Using individual testimonies, *New York Magazine* offers some illustrative examples of 12 young adults who did not vote in the midterm election in the United States in October 2018 (New York Magazine 2018). One of them, 21-year-old Drew, feels appalled that politicians, regardless of party, have not considered his interests. He voices his frustration in the following words:

> Millennials don't vote because a lot of politicians are appealing to older voters. We deserve politicians that are willing to do stuff for our future instead of catering to people who will not be here for our future. I'm a poli-sci major, so talking about politics is a daily thing for me. Half of the people I talk to seem very into voting. The other half are people who, like me, don't really feel represented.

The feeling among youth that government decisions are not legitimate is likely to be even larger in non-Western parts of the world, and this feeling of illegitimacy might fuel much more disruptive outcomes there. For instance, in the Middle East and North Africa, the so-called MENA region, countries tend to have large youth populations (as a share of the full population) with a median age under 30 or 25 years, depending on the country. Yet these same countries are home to some of the oldest legislators. For example, the median age in the Moroccan parliament in 2016 was 57 years, nearly 30 years more than the median age in the population. Focusing on Egypt, Nevens (2012) discusses the potential connections between frustration among the young, the unwillingness of the political class to allow youth to participate in the formal political system, and the probability of mass protests. As an illustration, she notes that in the 2010 elections, 67 percent of young adult Egyptians abstained from voting, and just one year later youth led the protests that ousted the old regime. This reflects a larger trend in the years 2011 and 2012 across the Middle East, with emerging protests in countries with autocratic leaders, such as Bahrain, Libya, Syria, Tunisia, and Yemen. While these protests varied from country to country, they all shared a specific component: "one noticeable similarity has been the huge numbers of young faces in the crowds; they are young men and women writing the slogans, shouting the loudest, and often bearing the brunt of the brutalities" (Nevens 2012, 45). Yet after the Arab Spring, surviving and emerging governments prevented young adults' inclusion again. For example, in Egypt many members of the youth movement, who had chosen to join new political parties in the direct aftermath of the Tahir Square protest, found themselves sidelined or allowed themselves to be sidelined for older and "more experienced" generations. Even young people working for El-Ghad, Ayman Nour's liberal opposition party, complained of "the sidelining of youth issues and the strict age-orientated hierarchical structure" (Nevens 2012, 46).

Communicative Mistrust

What is communicative mistrust? Using Mansbridge's framework, we understand it as a dysfunctional or seriously circumscribed communication between the out-group and in-group. Applied to youth, we can speak of a "communication gap," as Mansbridge (2015) labels it, if the older elite in different settings does not take young adults' voices seriously. We believe that a column in the newspaper *Washington Examiner* (2018) shows one example of such circumscription of communication. The column refers to the "March for Our Lives" on the 24th of March 2018—one of the largest youth protests in North America since the Vietnam War protests, where hundreds of simultaneous student-led demonstrations voiced their support in favor of legislation to prevent gun violence in the United States. Actors in the political and media class met this protest with ridicule. For instance, a news' commentator dismissed youths' criticism of the gun lobby by saying, "Sorry, kids, that's not how politics works."[9]

The belittling of young adults in the political sphere can have serious consequences, including subconscious effects. Because peoples' surroundings inform how they view politics, it is likely that the societal discourse of youth as "unfit" for office will trickle down to a negative self-perception. In Trantidis's (2016, 152) words, "barriers to entry are hidden and involve long-standing yet often unspoken social biases that may go as far as to affect the group's self-perception of political capacity and, depending on the specific configuration of prevalent norms and attitudes, may create an environment of political disengagement that appears, on the surface, voluntary." It is plausible that when young adults perceive politics as something they should not take part in, the view of formal politics as distant to themselves may become stronger.

Of course, in most countries youth do not face sidelining from societal communication in the same way as African Americans did during segregation or Black South Africans during apartheid. In most countries, young adults have more or less the same rights as senior citizens, and youth issues such as education, same-sex marriage, or gun laws are discussion topics within society. Therefore we do not see trends of outright communicative mistrust between age cohorts in the general population. However, we do think there are indications of mistrust among young adults toward actors in establishment politics: youths' views do not always have the same weight, they are subdued in subtle ways, and political and social elites frequently belittle these voices.

Failure Elsewhere in the System of Representation

Descriptive representation is not the only means to make one's voice heard. To look at a disadvantaged group's overall discrimination, it is important to unravel whether this group has other means of representation in the

---

9. Yet we also note that there was a contrasting reaction to these protests. For instance, some actors argued as a response that it was time to extend the franchise in the United States to 16-year-old citizens (e.g., Bouie 2018).

political system of a country. Mansbridge (2015, 266) notes that "the most important contextual question to ask in determining the relative importance of descriptive representation may be simply how well the larger representative system represents a group's interests through mechanisms other than descriptive representation." We therefore try to disentangle how well the larger political system represents the interests of youth as a group through other channels of influence. In doing so, we have identified at least three possible venues in which youth could influence politics: youth wings in political parties, youth organizations and conferences, and student unions. However, we find that none of these groupings has sufficient power to influence the political system in a sustainable way.

First, youth wings in political parties can fill several goals. In Western democracies, they are generally a source of attracting talented people, nurturing promising career politicians, and forming an obedient party line (Heidar 2006; de Roon 2020).[10] Hooghe et al. (2004) suggest that elected politicians often have a background in these organizations.[11] Moreover, members in youth wings of political parties are often prone to having a more positive outlook of their capacity to exert influence through conventional politics than youth in general (Rainsford 2017, 2018). Yet the role of such wings in relation to the mother party varies in a range of features. These include the extent to which they can have their own position on policy issues, the size of their organization, and the capacity to exert influence within the main party (see Lamb 2002; Russel 2005; Mycock and Tonge 2012). Youth wings of political parties are important in that they allow young adults to make their first experiences in politics. Nevertheless, they cannot sufficiently represent youth. Because they only attract a fraction of youth in society, their power remains very limited and tend to be hampered by their dependency on the mother party.[12] In addition, not all (major) parties have youth wings as part of their party structures.

Second, youth organizations, conferences, and other civil society orga-

---

10. In authoritarian settings, such as Kenya, Cameroon, Malawi, and Zimbabwe, the purpose of youth wings is much less positive. In these settings, the mother party frequently creates these youth organizations to harass political opponents (Abbink 2005).

11. This literature has also studied the various motivations for why individuals join the youth wing of a political party (e.g., Bale et al. 2019; de Roon 2020; Weber 2020).

12. We also want to note that some countries—albeit very few—have witnessed the emergence of so-called youth parties, such as the National Youth Party of India. These parties are exclusively composed of young adults up to a certain age. Their mandate is to fight for the demands of the younger generations. Nevertheless, youth parties remain a very peripheral phenomenon, which does not affect the power balance in favor of youth.

nizations remain key arenas for adolescents and young adults to meet and formulate joint stands on various youth topics, such as the environment or education policies. Youth organizations and conferences lobby at all levels of government and in the international arena. Some umbrella organizations further foster the interests of youth. A prominent example is the European Youth Parliament, a politically unbound nonprofit organization, which has encouraged European youth to actively engage in citizenship for three decades now. Another national version of a model parliament is the United Kingdom Youth Parliament, which gathers children aged 11 to 18 years. A plethora of other national organizations exists in many countries, ranging from those of a more political flavor, such as youth environmental NGOs, to more cultural organizations such as church groups, sports associations, or social clubs. While prominent in collecting interests, neither model parliaments for adolescents and young adults nor youth organizations, in general, have prominent influence on the national and international level. While Turkie (2010) debates whether these associations get the "breadcrumbs from the table" of real influence, McGinley and Grieve (2010) state that for the local level, youth councils are rarely vested with meaningful power. In their words, "[y]outh councils allow limited involvement in decision-making, usually at the level of consultation rather than of encouraging young people to drive their own agenda" (260). In sum, we conclude that these youth organizations and conferences are, at present, not satisfactory in terms of increasing youth participation and representation.

Third, in most Western countries, universities have at least one student union, a body with some power to influence university politics. On college campuses, particularly in North America, student unions have an important function to fulfill. They aim at improving students' learning experiences, place emphasis on student engagement, and offer extracurricular activities to students (Brooks et al. 2015). They also try to influence university politics in a range of issues, including tuition fees and working conditions for student assistants. For example, in North America special unions for graduate students try to influence pay and working conditions for master's and doctoral students. There is also an undeniable link between student politics and general politics outside the campus, for instance in issues related to higher education, such as student loans and debt, affordable housing, and the right to free information.

There is a tendency of university campuses to generate political protests, especially in authoritarian settings (Dahlum and Wig 2021). Thinking about events such as the Tiananmen Square protests of 1989, the Arab Spring in

2010/11 or the more recent antigovernment protests in Hong Kong, students have been able to oppose rulers in some settings and periods collectively. Yet in most countries students and student unions are no longer powerful players outside educational institutions (Shah et al. 2017). In the current third decade of the 21st century, the 1968-era of youth activism—where students and student unions in places such as France, Germany, Mexico, and the United States brought their message of peace, equality (between the sexes), and the renewal of ideas and governments to society—is long gone. With decreased membership, the most these student unions can do today is to lobby their cause. In the 21st century, their influence in university matters such as tuition fees is limited at best, and beyond university matters they are a voice to which society hardly listens. For this reason, we cannot see student unions as a sufficiently large actor to influence politics systematically. In addition, their ability to influence society as a whole has limitations, considering that youth outside the university have no access to these unions.

2.3. Benefits and Costs of Increased Descriptive Representation of Youth

Overall, we do not find that young adults have strong channels or mechanisms of influence outside the representative system. It generally seems that in all five categories or contexts that Mansbridge (1999, 2015) discusses, the system of representative democracy does not fully integrate young adults. (1) Youth as a group have some uncrystallized substantive interests that are not represented in the system. (2) The political culture in many countries perceives them as unfit to rule. (3) Youth have, in several settings, the widespread feeling that the system lacks legitimacy. (4) At least in the political sphere there is some communicative mistrust between younger citizens and the more senior political elites (even if this communicative mistrust might not be present between age cohorts when it comes to the nonpolitical world). (5) Youth also lack alternative mechanisms of representation in the system. For these reasons, an application of Mansbridge's theoretical framework would lend support to the argument that we should accept costs of descriptive representation for youth as a group (see table 1). Young (1989, 265) confirms this observation. According to her, young people are one of a number of groups in the United States that ought to be "clear candidates for group representation in policy making." We find it plausible that this assessment of the United States is also relevant for most countries across

Table 1. Schematic illustration of when to accept the costs of descriptive representation

Context for youth	Fulfillment of criteria
Uncrystallized substantive interests	Yes
Historically seen as "unfit to rule"	Yes
Diminished legitimacy of government decisions	Yes
Communicative mistrust	Partly
Failures elsewhere in system of representation	Yes

the globe. The United States is a prime example, but by far not the only one, of a country with a political class that tends to consist of older people. When we compare youths' representation in parliaments with their representation in society, young adults lacking representation is a feature of nearly every country. This lack of representation feeds into the processes of what we label a vicious cycle of youth alienation in politics.

2.4. The Vicious Cycle of Political Alienation

The underrepresentation of young adults is problematic on several fronts. There are strong arguments to support the conclusion that youth ought to have a larger presence in decision-making bodies. Yet, beyond the normative argument, there is also a broader, more empirical, problem generated by low levels of youth representation. The relative absence of young adults in assemblies feeds into a larger cycle of political alienation (Pruitt 2017). Aside from a lack of representation, this larger cycle (see figure 2) consists of two more elements: first, that youth in the 21st century tend to have low levels of political interest and knowledge, and second, that they are less likely than other adults to participate in conventional political activities. The literature has extensively researched these latter two components of the vicious circle of political alienation, but it lacks a thorough discussion of the underrepresentation of youth in political office.

2.4.1. Youths' Lack of Political Interest and Knowledge

Political interest is at the center of nearly all types of political engagement. Verba and colleagues (1995, 345) note that "citizens who are interested in politics—who follow politics, who care about what happens, who are concerned with who wins and loses—are more likely to be politically active." Yet today's youth are in many aspects a generation of "political dropouts," with

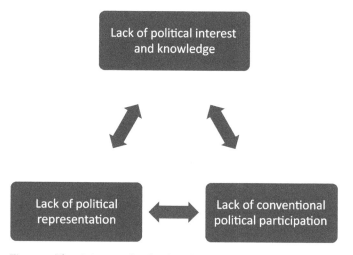

Figure 2. The vicious cycle of political alienation of young adults

little interest in conventional politics (Milner 2010). Trends from the United States and elsewhere suggest that young adults born in the 1980s and 1990s show distressingly low levels of interest in establishment-oriented forms of politics (Lupia and Philpot 2005). In the words of Soule (2001, 4):

> Over the past forty years, no generation has begun with such low levels of interest in politics. Cross-sectional surveys of incoming freshmen reveal that only 26% consider it very important or essential to keep up to date with political affairs. This is a near record low, in contrast to over 50% of students prior to 1970 and 42% in 1990.

There are worrying signs that many young adults today are simply not engaged in current affairs and do not follow the news. For example, David Mindich's 2005 book, *Tuned Out: Why Americans under 40 Don't Follow the News,* paints a rather gloomy picture of a young generation more invested in the TV series *American Idol* than the presidential debates. Somewhat less provocatively, his study presents ample evidence from the early 2000s of youth having abandoned traditional news (political news from newspapers, magazines, television, and the Internet). More recent works on the interests of young adults in politics (e.g., Martin 2012b; Barrett and Pachi 2019) largely mirror these trends of declining levels of political interest.[13]

---

13. Needless to say, this literature reports heterogeneity in political interest among the group of youth, which is explained by, among others, gender differences (e.g., Pfanzelt

This tendency for youth to have relatively low interest in politics frequently connects to their lack of political knowledge. Political knowledge is quintessential to participate in the political process; individuals must have the political information necessary to comprehend complex political realities, the ability to assimilate and organize such information, and the motivation to do so (Luskin 1990). In other words, without basic knowledge, citizens cannot situate themselves within the political spectrum, they understand neither the party programs nor nuanced policy proposition, and they might not understand the stakes of elections (Howe 2010; Wattenberg 2015). In a range of contexts, youth are in this situation today. At least in the Western world, they do not know much about formal politics. They generally do not know the key political figures and have gaps in their knowledge of how the representative system around them works. For example, about 50 percent of young Canadians do not know whether the national government or the provincial government is responsible for education, defense, the postal service, and fiscal policies (Stockemer and Rocher 2017). Youth in other countries including the United States, Germany, and the United Kingdom have equally low rates of functional political knowledge (which measures how the system works) and factual political knowledge (which gauges whether people know political facts or persons) (Faas 2007; Hoskins et al. 2015).

2.4.2. Youths' Lack of Conventional Political Participation

Electoral Turnout

Not only do young adults across the globe tend to be less prone to turn out to vote in elections than those from the older generations (Grasso 2014) but they also vote less than previous generations of young adults (see Goerres 2007; Sloam 2013). In fact, besides education, age is probably the most established individual-level factor predicting a person's probability of voting (see Blais 2000).[14] As an example of this increased disengagement, Blais and Loewen (2011) find that from the 1960s to the 2000s, turnout rates of newly eligible voters in Canada dropped from 70 to 40 percent. Holbein and

---

and Spies 2019), political socialization (e.g., Abendschoen 2013), and the amount of discussions young adults have with family and friends (e.g., Dostie-Goulet 2009).

14. As a nuance, Bhatti et al. (2012) suggest that besides a small decrease after the years following a person's enfranchisement, the relationship between turnout and age is largely curvilinear, with people in the younger cohorts generally significantly less likely to participate than those in their 50s and 60s.

Hillygus (2016) focus on the low turnout rates among young Americans. They report that the group of people aged 18 to 24 years voted at a rate of about 50 percent in 1972, whereas people above 25 years had a participation rate of approximately 70 percent. By 2012, 40 years later, youth turnout had dropped by 9 points to about 41 percent, whereas turnout of those older than 25 years merely dropped by 5 points to 65 percent (see also Holbein and Hillygus 2020). While the youth turnout literature is the largest in the context of the United States, findings in other countries seem to mirror those in America. Low turnout rates among younger cohorts of the population are a feature in settings as diverse as Australia (Hannan-Morrow and Roden 2014), Britain (Henn and Foard 2012), Chile (Acuña-Duarte 2017), Greece (Sloam 2013), South Africa (Scott et al. 2011), and Taiwan (Achen and Wang 2019), to mention a few.

Electoral Campaigns and Electoral Appeals

There is reason to believe that the political elite across contexts are aware that older voters tend to participate in elections at a higher rate than younger ones. In the United States, there is an established concern between the two major parties to safeguard the support from the older generations. As Ansolabehere noted in the wake of the 2018 mid-term elections for the House of Representatives, "[b]oth parties have to do well with the senior vote if they are going to do well in the general election" (quoted in Bunis 2018). Conversely, the low turnout of youth has implications for how interested parties are in addressing their concerns. Berry noted in 2014 that the contrasting rates of participation of young and old voters is "a fact not lost on the electoral strategists employed by the mainstream political parties" (708). In the words of Davidson and Binstock (2011, 26), "[p]oliticians are wary of 'waking a sleeping giant' of angry older voters. They strive to position themselves in a fashion that they think will appeal to the self-interests of older voters, and usually take care that their opponents do not gain an advantage in this arena." Electoral pollsters label this strategy to target the subsection of older voters that of *segmentation* (see Bannon 2004). This strategy is apparent both in how and on which policies parties target older voters. In the United States, for instance, both major parties have made use of senior citizen committees, "senior desks," and other structures designed to target older voters (Binstock 2012). To our knowledge, comparable "youth desks" do not exist. An example from the United Kingdom on how party actors have attempted to target older people and make them unite across party lines is the framing of Labour's health-care reform in 2010 as a "death tax" by the Conservatives (Davidson and Binstock 2011). While some election campaigns have involved targeted attempts by political actors to make young voters rally for a certain candidate, such as in the 2015 Canadian federal election (The Star 2015), the literature generally does not suggest that parties see young voters as the same decisive factor as the "senior vote."

Party Organizations

The rates of interest, knowledge, and different modes of participation suggest that youth are not very likely to engage themselves in established party organizations. For example, works by Rainsford (2018), as well as Bale and colleagues (2019), note that the average member of a political party is generally much older than the average voter in the population. Studies in settings such as Denmark (see Pedersen et al. 2004), Ireland (see Gallagher and Marsh 2004), Great Britain (see Seyd and Whiteley 2004; Scarrow and Gezgor 2010), Canada (see Cross and Young 2004), and Sweden (see Kölln 2017) confirm the old age of party members; there too party members are very seldom young adults.[15] In fact, the few young individuals who join political parties tend to be politically socialized by their parents; more often than others, they are exposed to political information as children and tend to have experienced partisan activity through their parents' activism (Bruter and Harrisson 2009).

2.5. The Threefold Link between Young Adults' Low Political Interest and Knowledge, Their Low Electoral Participation, and Their Lack of Representation in Office

So far we have shown that young citizens' increasing political alienation renders the voice of young adults less important because parties and candidates gain relatively little from catering to the interests of a group that largely refrains from voting (Van Parijs 1998; Delli Carpini 2000; Henn and Foard 2012). This feeds into parties' strategies for recruitment to political office; they have less of an incentive to nominate younger candidates. Yet, in line with Norris and Lovenduski (1993, 1995), we believe that the supply

---

15. The 2016 United Nations Global Youth Report confirms these observations. The report shows that political party membership is less prevalent among those under the age of 30 than among older adults (United Nations 2016a).

of young candidates for office matters for their political presence. The equation is quite simple: if there are no young candidates, there cannot be any young legislators.

A recent experimental meta-study on age and candidate preferences by Eshima and Smith (2022) documents that voters across age groups generally prefer younger candidates over older ones. This suggests that the explanation for the gerontocracy we witness in current politics is not about whether voters accept young leaders. The questions are therefore: do young adults show a distressingly low interest in running for office (see Lupia and Philpot 2005)? Do parties ignore young adults? Or do they use them as fillers? There is some evidence that youth are either reluctant to run or face some formal or informal barriers precluded from running. For example, Prihatini (2019) compares the age distribution of the national population of Indonesia with the structure of the candidate pool in the country running for parliament. She finds that the group of people aged 20 to 29 years constitute about a sixth of the nation's populace. However, this group makes up only 5 percent of the people in the group of candidates. Lawless and Fox (2015) confirm this observation for the United States; the two scholars report that young people have generally low interest in running for office. Shames's (2017) study also echoes this finding for graduates from top educational institutions, traditionally a recruiting ground for politicians. Accordingly, this segment of young adults views the system as corrupted by expensive campaigns and hysteric media attention often associated with elections in the country. Instead they express a wish to make a change through other ways of political engagement. In sum, the literature is nearly unanimous that young candidates under 30 years old are somewhat of an anomaly in the candidacy pool. Yet our empirical analysis (see chapter 6) illustrates that in some countries such as Switzerland youth run in quite high numbers, but this willingness to run does not translate into adequate representation.

2.6. The Endemic Nature of the Vicious Cycle of Youths' Political Alienation

The literature on political participation has established a clear link that low political interest feeds into youths' lack of participating in conventional politics. We add that both of these features should influence youths' underrepresentation in elected and selected assemblies. Yet there is discussion on whether this vicious cycle of alienation only relates to conventional forms of participation of young adults (Dermody et al. 2010). The starting point of this debate is whether the young generation is apathetic or, rather, engaged in other modes of politics. Several scholars (e.g., Mycock and Tonge 2012; Thijssen et al. 2016) argue that youth are turning their back on formal politics, but that this alienation should not be equated to disengagement in political issues. Rather, in the view of Norris (2002), we witness a transformation away from formal and traditional forms of engagement, such as being member in a political party and voting, to new types of participation such as Internet activism and consumer-oriented activism (see also Dalton 2008; Martin 2012a). Marsh et al. (2007, 39) explain this transformation eloquently: "The failure of individuals to participate in the formal political arena, by voting, joining a political party or demonstrating, is not usually a sign of apathy. Rather, it may reflect alienation from a political system which is biased against them."

We do not disagree with this more nuanced conclusion, given that there are signs of greater engagement of youth on a variety of issues including climate change, consumer politics, and antigun protests (in the United States). We also agree that many "young people are concerned about matters that are essentially 'political' in nature such as the environment, but these concerns lie beyond the boundaries of how politics is conventionally understood" (Henn 2002, 168). Again, in the words of Henn, we think that some members of the younger generations "are 'engaged sceptics'—they are interested in political affairs, but distrustful of those who are elected to positions of power and charged with running the political system" (187). We also wholeheartedly agree with Dalton (2008), who states that we should not equate the fact that young adults tend to reject voter participation in high numbers with a generation without values of engagement and tolerance that has the potential to make them good citizens. Grasso (2014) summarizes this somewhat brighter perspective by stating:

> From consumer politics, to community campaigns, to international networks facilitated by online technology; from the ballot box, to the street, to the Internet; from political parties, to social movements and issue groups, to social networks. There is overwhelming evidence to show that young people are not apathetic about politics—they have their own views and engage in a wide variety of ways (664).

Yet we do not concur with a rather optimistic account of politics that sees modern "politics" as something different from traditional politics (see Pontes et al. 2018). That is, we simply do not see these feedback loops between new forms of political engagement and participation in traditional conventional politics for the large majority of youth. If these feedback loops were widespread, then we would likely see higher rates of voting, party membership, and degrees of political knowledge for the age cohort of young adults. As far as we can tell, however, this potential feedback from new modes of participation to conventional modes is just not large enough to make any meaningful difference. While engaged youth, who are leaders in all sorts of political action, surely exist, these young adults seem to be a small group (see Melo and Stockemer 2014). The majority of young people participate less in formal politics today than 30 years ago; they have less political interest and knowledge, and youth today have only a marginal voice in the decision-making bodies that matter.

There are several reasons why formal politics matter. Voting in elections is still one of the most established forms of political action, parties remain the main political actors, and parliaments and cabinets the places where laws are drafted, decided, and implemented. Therefore it matters *where* youth participate (Rainsford 2017), and it is worrying that young adults tend to opt out from established channels of participation. We find this to be a concern since it highlights that young adults experience feelings of alienation toward the system of representative democracy. Moreover, it is highly problematic if youth sense that "politicians and political institutions are not interested in their concerns and interests and do not address their needs" (Barrett and Pachi 2019, 7). Marsh et al. (2007, 218) summarize the problem as follows:

> Disengagement from electoral processes among young people flags deeper problems of the lack of responsiveness of political representative institutions to citizens and especially to young people, who are rarely directly addressed by politicians even in relation to issues that directly affect them. Instead, there are intense debates *about* young people, which tend to focus on anti-social behavior, educational deficits, drugs, crime and so on in ways that rarely acknowledge the perspectives of young people themselves.

If this negative cycle of youth marginalization in politics has adverse effects in Western societies, its effects are potentially even more harmful outside Europe and the United States. The relative absence of youth in parliaments has dramatic repercussions in low-income societies where the demographic trends form a "bulge," that is, children and young adults comprise a large share of the country's population.[16] Textbooks on development in Africa tend to portray this demographic phenomenon as a key challenge for the continent because of its connections to mass unemployment among young adults and the implications for social instability (see Mills et al. 2017).[17] Importantly, Abbink (2005, 1) notes that young adults in Africa "are growing up in conditions of mass employment and are facing exclusion. . . . They also are marginalized in nationalized state policies and have a weak legal position."

In more detail, African countries provide numerous examples of settings with old leaders and young electorates. For instance, countries in the Middle East and Africa tend to have a large youth population (as a share of the full population), yet these countries are home to some of the legislatures with the oldest representatives in the world. This is partly because "older generations" of African leaders clung to power after decolonization (Abbink 2005). Frustrated youth, in whose eyes the senior (and often autocratic) leaders lost all legitimacy to govern, were often instrumental during fights against oppression, such as the anti-apartheid movement in South Africa (van Kessel 2000) or the Arab Spring in 2010–2011. Yet, after these fights, neither the old elites, when they stayed in power, nor the new elites when they have formed new governing coalitions have invited youth to join the new governments. Just to name one country, Egypt, was a case, where the political elites marginalized young adults in the postuprising world.

This sidelining is not to say that youth are not important to political parties. Rather in many African countries (and probably elsewhere as well), "the political elites see the youth as an important constituency for electoral mobilization because of their sheer numbers, their availability, and their eagerness to take up anything that may relieve them of conditions of poverty" (Bob-Milliar 2014, 39). However, they also try to manipulate them so that they do not reach the pinnacle of power. As such, political elites in several African countries have found ways to include young adults in lower-ranked positions. For instance, in some settings with widespread political clientelism, such as Ghana, party elites convince youth party activists to engage in small-scale yet intense electoral manipulation (Bob-Milliar 2014). Elites in such settings might have incentives to pay lip service and include young adults in their leadership, yet it seems they only

---

16. Such patterns are often linked to development where a country achieves success in reducing infant mortality, but mothers still have a high fertility rate (Lin 2012).

17. The literature on violent conflicts (e.g., Urdal 2006) and uprisings (e.g., LaGraffe 2012) generally studies youth bulges.

do so very strategically as not to threaten the power of the dominant and elderly elite (Abbink 2005).

2.7. Increased Youth Representation: One Way to Break the Vicious Cycle of Youth Alienation

For us, the linkages between youths' low interest in formal politics, their limited degree of participation, and their insufficient levels of representation are evident. We agree with Delli Carpini (2000, 344), who outlined the problem youth faced two decades ago in a way that we think is still valid today:

> [M]ost of the formal institutions of public life either ignore young adults and the issues that matter to them or are ill equipped to attract young adults and provide them with meaningful opportunities to participate. Parties and candidates see little reason to devote their resources to reaching out to young Americans given that this age cohort is less likely to vote than older Americans. Government officials are unlikely to listen to young Americans, knowing there is little risk that they will be punished for their neglect at the polls.

Lupia and Philpot (2005, 1123) suggest that there are ways to *break* such a vicious circle: "If political institutions, candidates, and organizations can present politics in ways that are more relevant to young voters, the current decline in their political interest levels may be slowed, stopped, or perhaps even reversed." But how can we make politics more relevant to young adults? We propose that one way to bring young adults back to conventional politics is to focus on one key aspect of the problem: the absence of youth in political assemblies. Echoing Briggs (2017), we believe that young adults today will have a difficult time relating to politics if they are absent from the ranks of representatives and if their views are ignored completely, or at least sidelined: "Little wonder, therefore, that many young people do seem to regard the political arena as alien territory" (Briggs 2017, 1). Coleman (2017) makes another compelling point for increased youth representation by switching the perspective. According to him, the young adults of today have not abandoned politics. Rather there is a disconnect between the contemporary political culture and the perspectives and interests of the young. Similarly, Loader (2007) suggests that the political representatives in power are disengaged from the reality of young adults and unable to sympathize with young people's experiences.

Increasing young adults' political representation could be beneficial on several grounds. Granting the young adequate representation could break the vicious cycle of youth alienation. For example, younger cohorts could bring their topics of importance to the political agenda, which in turn could entice young adults to participate in the political process. In more detail, we can see at least three possible ways that increasing youth representation could have a positive influence on other modes of political participation and youths' substantive representation. First, it could trigger higher youth turnout. Second, it could ensure that the interests of the young gain access to parliament and other elected and nonelected bodies. Third, it could entice parties and politicians to alter their agendas and adopt more policies important to young adults. While these assumptions are difficult to prove through a definitive empirical test, we have good reasons to believe in the validity of these claims, as we outline in the sections below.

2.7.1. The Link between Greater Numbers of Young Candidates and Higher Youth Turnout

Of course, this larger question is difficult to answer. Social identity theory holds that younger voters, subconsciously, have a natural tendency to identify with younger candidates (Ben-Bassat and Dahan 2012). In a recent experimental setting, Shen and Shoda (2021) suggest that young people are more likely than older ones to prefer younger politicians. Taken together, this mechanism would imply that a) young voters are more likely to vote for young candidates and, by extension, b) youth could potentially mobilize in higher numbers when young politicians are running for elections.

Empirically, the first of these two predictions is difficult to test. Because of the secrecy of the ballot, it is inherently difficult to investigate whether young voters vote for younger politicians. In most exit polls during elections, pollsters ask respondents about which party they voted for, rather than which candidate. While not direct, there is some anecdotal evidence suggesting that youth are more likely to support younger politicians. As Sevi (2021) discusses, the examples of the election of Barack Obama or Justin Trudeau are prime illustrations where young voters tend to support young leaders. Of course, there are also contrasting examples when youth supported the election older politicians. Jeremy Corbyn in the United Kingdom and Jean-Luc Mélenchon in France would be examples of this latter phenomenon. Yet young voters did not turn to these politicians because of their (old) age or experience but rather because they represent most closely their beliefs. Therefore these examples illustrate that there is certainly not a deterministic congruence between the age of voters and their preferred electoral choice.

Nevertheless, there is more and more evidence from surveys in support of the claim that younger voters prefer young politicians. For instance, Saglie et al. (2015) suggest that there is a linkage in the voting preference of young citizens. Focusing on Norway, the authors suggest that young citizens generally select young candidates across the country through preference votes. In other words, these scholars illustrate that the increase in young politicians winning a local council seat is likely not due to any proactive nominations by parties but rather driven by young voters, who cast their ballot for young candidates. Through a comparative perspective, and building on ideas of "affinity voting," Sevi (2021) tests the expectation that voters prefer and vote for leaders that are closer to them in age. Analyzing surveys across Western countries, she shows that increased distance in age between a leader and voter reduces the likelihood that the voter will have a favorable opinion about the leader and vote for her party.

Likewise, while it is difficult to evaluate whether having younger legislators entices more young citizens to turn out on election day, there are suggestive findings in this direction. For example, the work of Pomante and Schraufnagel (2015) supports this stipulation empirically through two types of analyses. First, the authors show in an experiment that stated intentions to vote increase among young U.S. adults when there are younger politicians in the candidate pool. Second, the authors confirm this hypothetical scenario with observational data on gubernatorial and Senate elections in U.S. states. In more detail, their study finds that youth turn out to vote in greater numbers when politicians are younger and the age difference between candidates is larger (i.e., young voters are more likely to cast their ballot when there is a clear age difference between candidates and young voters can make a deliberate choice in favor of a young representative). More indirectly, through case study evidence in the United States, Ulbig and Waggener (2011) discover that even the age of the person who registers young people matters. In more detail, the two scholars find that youth who are registered to vote by other young adults participate in elections at higher rates than young adults registered by older individuals.

2.7.2. The Degree to Which Young Politicians Represent Young Voters

In the current climate of political alienation, young adults doubt politicians' ability to represent them. In the words of Henn et al. (2002, 178), youth in the United Kingdom are "highly skeptical of the notion that political parties and elected representatives genuinely seek to further young peoples' interests and act upon their concerns." Does this skepticism change if more young adults are in elected and nonelected political office? The KOLFU-data, a unique survey sent to all of Sweden's 10,000-plus local politicians, with a response rate of about 70 percent (see Karlsson and Gilljam 2014), offers some preliminary evidence suggesting that, compared to older representatives, younger ones might be more attuned to the needs of the young. In more detail, the survey records register-based data on the birthdates of all politicians and poses the following question to local politicians that hold office at the municipal or regional level in Sweden: "How important is the following task to you personally as a councilor?" One of the subitems to this question was: "Advance the interests and opinions of the young." We can see that answers to this question vary with the age of a politician. Among politicians aged 18–34, the percentage of respondents stating that this is "very important" is about 44 percent. Yet the share of affirmative answers decreases substantially in each age group; among politicians aged 35–49, 50–64, and 65 and above, the shares are 36 percent, 34 percent and 31 percent, respectively.[18]

2.7.3. The Degree to Which Young Politicians Support Policies Important to Young Adults

The literature on representation of women and ethnic minorities holds that the interests of these groups are better reflected among representatives that belong themselves to these groups. For example, in an experimental study Mendelberg et al. (2014) find that we need a critical mass of women in decision-making bodies so that women can voice and push through distinctive concerns pertaining to the family, children, and redistributive politics. Focusing on another out-group, LGBTQ people, Hansen and Treul (2015) highlight that LGBTQ legislators can positively influence symbolic (low-cost gestures and actions) and substantive representation (laws regulating the rights of the LGBTQ community).

We have reason to assume that the same will be true for young politicians as well. First, there is growing research illustrating that young politicians behave differently in the legislative arena than their more senior col-

---

18. The relationship between politicians' age and their affirmation to represent the interests of the young is significant when running a simple chi-square test of independence (p < .000).

leagues.[19] Second, and more importantly, there is some direct evidence that more young politicians in positions of power lead to different policies. In support of this claim, McClean (2019) uses data on mayoral candidates in Japan (2004–2017). With the help of a regression discontinuity design, he shows that younger mayors increase spending on child welfare more than older mayors, both in absolute and relative terms. Conversely, Curry and Haydon (2018) demonstrate that older lawmakers in the U.S. Congress are more likely to introduce legislation on certain senior issues, primarily those that are less publicly salient, compared to younger colleagues.

We want to bolster the claim of a link between descriptive and substantive representation with a short empirical example. In detail, we look at voting records of legislators in the U.S. House of Representatives (see table 2), highlighting that there is an effect from being a young representative on the tendency to support stricter environmental legislation, while controlling for party affiliation, gender, and newcomer status. To illustrate, we use data from the nonprofit League of Conservation Voters (LCV),[20] which collects information on the individual voting record of the most important environmental bills.[21] The data we retrieved covers the second session of the 115th Congress (2018–2019) and evaluates the voting record of all representatives. We focus on legislators in the House of Representatives and our dependent variable is the percentage a legislator voted proenvironmentally (in favor of stricter regulations across environmental issues). As such, this measure ranges from 0 to 100 (0 indicates that the legislator never voted for stricter environmental legislation and 100 implies that they always voted for stricter regulation).

To capture whether there is an effect from being a young legislator on

19. For instance, research suggests that, compared to more senior politicians, young politicians are often more successful in attracting public funds from central governments before elections (see Alesina et al. 2019). They are also more active in terms of legislative activities (Ono 2015; but see Hajek [2019] for a contrasting suggestion) as well as more likely to rebel against party policy positions (see Nemoto et al. 2008; Meserve et al. 2009).
20. The nonprofit League of Conservation Voters (LCV) publishes a National Environmental Scorecard every Congress since 1970. It provides objective, factual information about the most important environmental legislation considered and the corresponding voting records of all members of the House of Representatives. This scorecard represents the consensus of experts from about 20 respected environmental and conservation organizations who selected the key votes on the most important issues of the year, including energy, climate change, public health, public lands, and wildlife conservation, and spending for environmental programs.
21. The LCV data has high reliability, and several scholarly works use this variable as outcome variables (see, e.g., Fredriksson and Wang 2011; Kim and Urpelainen 2017).

Table 2. The influence of age on the voting records in favor of stricter environmental protection among members of the U.S. House of Representatives (Tobit regression analysis)

	Coefficient
Aged 40 or under	6.93**
	(2.94)
Republican	−86.38***
	(1.65)
Freshmen	1.27
	(2.48)
Women	3.86
	(2.03)
Constant	89.26***
	(1.36)
Log Likelihood	−1459.54
N	435

Standard errors in parentheses, *p < .10, **p < .05, ***p < .01 (two tailed).

the voting patterns in regard to environmental regulations, we created a binary measure (coded 1 for young politicians aged 40 years or under, and 0 otherwise). We also consider alternative explanations that could affect the outcome of this variable and include three control variables in our model (party affiliation, newcomer effects, and gender). In more detail, we add a dichotomous measure for *Party affiliation* (coded 1 for Republicans and 0 for Democrats), a dichotomous variable for *Freshmen* (coded 1 for freshmen and 0 for incumbents and those who have held a seat in the House before), and a dichotomous indicator for *Women*, coded 1 (and 0 denoting men). Because the data is truncated (i.e., 77 Republicans earned a 0 percent and 29 Democrats earned a perfect score of 100 percent), we use Tobit regression techniques that are better suited to deal with truncated and censored data than regular OLS.[22]

Table 2 shows that age matters in explaining whether a legislator votes in favor of environmental protection or not. The regression analysis predicts that members of the House of Representatives aged 40 years or under are, on average, and controlling for their party affiliation, seven percentage points more likely to vote proenvironmentally than those who are at least 41 years old. In the hyperpartisan environment of the United States, where

---

22. The House Democratic Caucus averaged 90 percent, whereas the House Republican Caucus averaged 8 percent.

partisan affiliation trumps nearly all other factors, this is a significant figure. The effect size is also nearly double the size of the coefficient for gender. Hence our example provides support for our proposition that age matters in legislative behavior. We also deem it plausible that youths' absence in parliaments hurts not only legislation in favor of the environment but also other issues. For example, the dominance of the elderly in the U.S. Congress is probably one of the reasons that gun control legislation in the country has literally no chance of passing.

Some research from other contexts buttresses our assumption. There is some indirect and some direct evidence beyond the United States that young representatives are more likely to represent the interests of the young. More indirectly, Giger and Bernauer (2009) find in a cross-national sample that voters aged 18 to 30 years old are less likely than voters in their middle age to hold aligned views with the party they supported. This finding hints at the fact that there is less congruence in views between youth and party platforms than there is for older citizens. In the context of Switzerland, Kissau et al. (2012) examine how citizens' attitudes in different age cohorts relate to the median position in parliament. At least for some measures (e.g., the justification of torture and the harder punishment of criminals), citizens aged 21 to 30 are further away from the median legislator (which was over 50 years old at the time of the study) than those aged 51 to 60 years. More in favor of a direct link, recent work by Bailer and colleagues (2022) documents that young MPs are more active on youth-oriented issues than their older counterparts—at least during their first term in office. Yet with seniority, enthusiasm and activity in favor of youth issues declines.

Altogether these findings support our assumption that having a parliament of older cohorts of people likely tends to skew policy toward the interests of voters from this cohort (see also Van Parijs 1996). We also believe that more young people in positions of power could have a longer-term indirect effect on youths' substantive representation; it could change the cultures of political assemblies. For example, more youth in positions of power could give them more visibility. This implies that inside and outside the parliament, cabinet, or the state's bureaucracy, young MPs, cabinet members, and civil servants could talk about their priorities and those of their group—be it in the fields of education, equal rights for everyone, reproductive rights, the environment, or any other topic. In these discussions, the topic of youth political alienation might also become more prevalent, which might increase older MPs' awareness of these concerns, and they too might feel compelled to act, both on youth topics and to stop youths' lack of representation.

2.8. The Youth Representation Literature and Our Contribution

Youth today have a case to make for group representation in legislatures. More young people in positions of power will lead to more intergenerational justice and will correct inadequacies in representation. A larger presence of young adults (defined largely as individuals between 18 and 35 years, or 18 and 40) also has the potential to break or alleviate the vicious cycle of youths' political alienation. Yet empirically we do not know the whole magnitude of youths' underrepresentation. In fact, compared to other outgroups such as women, ethnic minorities, or LGBTQ people the literature on youth representation is quite scarce.

We can divide existing (empirical) studies on the underrepresentation of youth (e.g., Norris and Franklin 1997; Joshi 2013; Kissau et al. 2012; IPU 2014, 2018, 2021; Krook and Nugent 2018; Stockemer and Sundström 2018) into three types of analyses. First, and without providing any solid proof for such a claim, introductory handbooks to the study of government frequently state that legislators are normally middle-aged to senior (e.g., Blondel 2014, 257). Second, several case studies either explicitly or implicitly mention that there is an overrepresentation of middle-aged and senior individuals among legislators in a set of industrialized countries (see Norris 1997) or in specific countries, including France (Murray 2008), Sweden (Burness 2000), Switzerland (Kissau et al. 2012), and Ghana (Van Gyampo 2015). In more detail, these studies all confirm that the age group between 50 and 60 constitutes the largest share of elected legislators, and that the percentage of young parliamentarians tends to be in the single digits (regardless whether the respective study defined this age cohort as the percentage of MPs aged 30, 35, or 40 years or under).

Third, a handful of comparative studies explicitly discusses the representation of various age cohorts in parliament. For example, Narud and Valen (2000) compare age representation in the legislatures in the Nordic countries, confirming the overrepresentation of individuals in their 50s and 60s. Broadening the number of countries to 70, reports published by the Inter Parliamentary Union (IPU) in 2014, 2016, 2018, and 2021 confirm this finding. According to the IPU (2021), about half of the 110 lower houses of parliament examined have 2 percent or fewer young parliamentarians (defined as age 30 or younger). Even more pronounced, the same report finds that only ten of the 37 upper houses covered have anyone aged 30 or below in their chamber in 2020. The average representation of youth aged 30 and below is also at an infinitesimal .5 percent. There are also some studies, albeit few, that try to explain variation in the share of young legislators across countries. For example, in his study of 14 Asian countries, Joshi (2013) finds that proportional representation (PR) electoral systems render parliaments a bit more accessible for young politicians. In a follow up study on the characteristics of members of parliament (MPs) in Bangladesh, Bhutan, India, Nepal, Pakistan, and Sri Lanka, Joshi (2015) confirms that PR positively affects the descriptive parliamentary representation of young adults.

Building on these comparative pieces, Stockemer and Sundström (2018, 2019a) have published two articles, one on youths' representation in national parliaments using a global sample and another on young elected members in the European Parliament. Both articles point to the centrality of formal institutions in explaining variation in the average age of parliamentarians. Stockemer and Sundström (2018) confirm the finding in Joshi (2013, 2015) that PR increases the percentage of young legislators under the age of 35 and 40, respectively.[23] In addition, they concur with Krook and Nugent (2018), who point to the importance of another institution, namely that of age barriers for candidacy, which increase the average age among legislatures in a global sample.

Finally, several recent pieces discuss the representation of youth within an intersectionality perspective. These pieces come to a nuanced finding. For one, they assert that the presence of young women in today's legislatures is even smaller than that of young men (see Belschner and Garcia de Paredes 2020; Joshi and Och 2021). Yet this finding comes with the caveat that the gender gap in representation might actually be the smallest among young parliamentarians aged 35 years or under (see Stockemer and Sundström 2019b, 2019c, 2019d).

By providing a comprehensive perspective on youth representation in parliament and in cabinet, our book offers several contributions to the literature on youth descriptive representation. For example, while there are several studies (e.g., Joshi 2013, 2015; Krook and Nugent 2018; Stockemer and Sundström 2018) on youths' underrepresentation in parliament, there is so far no study on variation in youths' underrepresentation among political parties. The same applies to the cabinet; no study exists that provides a comprehensive overview of youths' numerical presence in ministerial portfolios. It is also unknown what type of portfolios young politicians typically occupy. When it comes to the parliament, this book adds to the current lit-

---

23. See also Sundström and Stockemer (2021), an article that introduces a new way to measure youth representation in a country, by capturing the ratio between the share of young adults among MPs and the share of young adults in the voting-age population.

erature as well. It includes more parliaments than any prior study and adds a diachronic perspective—that is, it offers some data on the development of youth representation over the past decades for four selected countries (i.e., Australia, France, Germany, and the United Kingdom). Moreover, we add an individual perspective on young adults that run for office by comparing young candidates to young representatives. Is the problem that youth do not gain representation one of too few candidates running or a consequence of the tendency that young candidates do not win? Finally, we add a micro-level perspective and present more in-depth research of young candidates and elected representatives from Sweden (a country with high youth representation) and Switzerland (a country with low youth representation). In more detail, we constructed an original survey, which we sent to successfully elected MPs as well as unsuccessful candidates, aiming to further uncover the factors that benefit and hinder youths' advancements in electoral positions.

CHAPTER 3

YOUTHS' UNDERREPRESENTATION IN NATIONAL PARLIAMENTS

Youth can be the leaders of tomorrow—if we procrastinate.

(FREECHILD INSTITUTE FOR YOUTH ENGAGEMENT 2019)

3.1. The Magnitude of Youths' Underrepresentation in Parliament

To determine the extent to which young adults face underrepresentation in parliament, we engaged in a large-scale data collection effort. We collected individual data on the age of elected politicians and then aggregated these data at the country level. Mostly, this individual information on the age of MPs came from the website EveryPolitician, which gathers and shares data on politicians' biographies, using information from parliaments' websites.[1] We complemented this information with original data for some countries by hand-coding the age of MPs from biographies on national parliaments' websites. For each country, we used data for the most recent parliament available. This gave us a sample of 131 parliaments from all continents with an election date between the years 2010 and 2019. The scope is larger than in any prior study on this theme. We also validated these web-scraped data with the information we manually retrieved from the website of several national parliaments, in countries such as Germany and France. While doing this validation check, we found that the age data from the site EveryPolitician is analogous to the data found on the national parliamentary websites or has only minor variation. After gathering all age data for each parliament, we aggregated the individual-level age data of parliamentarians and created four country-level variables: the median age of parliamentarians, the mean age of parliamentarians, the percentage of young legislators aged 35 years

---

1. The content presented on the EveryPolitican portal collects information on legislators on national websites; it consists of the scraped version of these parliamentary websites. It includes data for more than 78,000 politicians.

or under, and the percentage of young legislators aged 40 years or under. We use these measures to first present some univariate statistics on the age distribution across the world's parliaments, and then as dependent variables to explain variation in the presence of young parliamentarians across countries.

The first finding that stands out is that our opening quote summarizes youths' presence in national parliaments relatively well. Quite cynical, the quote illustrates that youth are the leaders of tomorrow, a period when they are older themselves. Regardless of which of our four measures we use, our sample of national parliaments shows a stark underrepresentation of young adults. The age of the average and median legislator is roughly 50.6 years. If we look at youth in particular, we find that young members of parliament, those aged 35 years or under, constitute a mere 9.35 percent of all legislators. If we consider our second measure of youth, legislators aged 40 years or under at the beginning of the respective parliament, this group makes up slightly more than 20 percent of parliamentarians (i.e., 20.02 percent). If we further compare the age structure of parliaments with the age structure of societies, the magnitude of youths' underrepresentation is flagrant. While the median age of citizens is 29.8 years, the median age of the world's parliaments is more than 20 years older, or more than 50 years. Even more pronounced, the share of citizens aged 35 years or under in the world's population was roughly 58 percent in 2019 (see Worldometers 2019). However, the percentage of legislators aged 35 years or under is less than 10 percent in our sample of 131 countries. If we only look at the voting-age population, the 18- to 35-year-olds make up approximately 28 percent of the world's population, nearly exactly three times as much as the share of young MPs in our dataset. Even if we compare young legislators aged 40 years or under in our dataset to the world's share of citizens aged 18 to 40, the underrepresentation of youth in parliament is roughly one to two relative to the world population (see Worldometers 2019).

Yet youths' descriptive underrepresentation in legislatures does not spread evenly throughout the world. Rather there is wide variation between countries in the percentage of young legislators they elect to their country's national parliament. For example, our global sample reveals that there are some legislatures, such as Bosnia and Herzegovina or Kosovo, with a mean and median age of 40 years (see fig. 3). Yet, in other settings, such as Turkey and Palau, the mean and median age hovers around 65 years. If we look more specifically at one of our measures of youth representation, the percentage of parliamentarians aged 35 years or under, we get a very sober

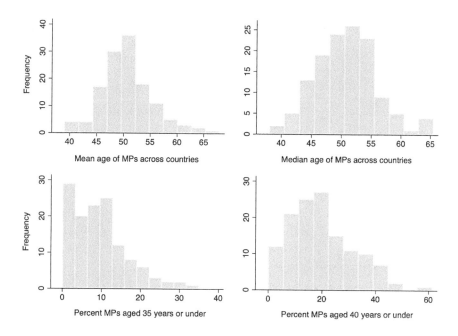

Figure 3. The age distribution in parliaments across the globe in or around 2019

picture. The mode in this distribution (i.e., the most frequently appearing value) is actually 0. In other words, 16 parliaments, or more than 12 percent of our 131 parliaments in total, do not have anybody in their ranks who was 35 years or younger at the time of election. This includes some of the countries with the youngest populations on the globe, such as Senegal and Malawi, where the median age in the population is under 20 years. Even if we look at the distribution of MPs aged 40 years or under, we still have six countries that have no legislator aged 40 years or under at the constitution of the parliament. These six countries are Botswana, Jamaica, Nauru, Palau, Saint Lucia, and Thailand.

On the brighter side, there are some countries with a significant share of young legislators (see table 3). For example, the median and average age is around 40 years in the two former Yugoslavian countries of Bosnia and Herzegovina and Kosovo. Another prime example is Armenia, where a majority of legislators was 40 years of age or under at the start of the legislative period. There are also some countries, such as San Marino and Ukraine, where the age

Table 3. Countries with the youngest parliaments

Mean age (years)	Bosnia and Herzegovina (39), Kosovo (39.58), Seychelles (40.03), Armenia (40.33), Haiti (42.51)
Median age (years)	Armenia (38), Bosnia and Herzegovina (39), Seychelles (41.5), Kosovo (42), San Marino (42)
Share of MPs 35 years or under (percent)	Armenia (34.85), Serbia (30.77), Kosovo (29.03), Seychelles (28.13), San Marino (23.43)
Share of MPs 40 years or under (percent)	Armenia (61.36), Kosovo (48.38), Seychelles (46.88), San Marino (42.85), Haiti (42.51)

Figure 4. The percent of MPs aged 35 years or under in legislatures across the globe

structure of parliament roughly mirrors the one in society. In fact, San Marino is an example where the parliament is younger than the population (i.e., the median age in parliament was 43.4 years at its inception in 2016, whereas the median age in the population this year was 44.7). Figures 4, 5, and 6 provide a snapshot of youths' representation across the globe.

3.2. Youth Representation in Legislatures over Time in Australia, Germany, France, and the United Kingdom

So far we have shown that young adults face severe underrepresentation in parliaments across the globe, but we do not know whether there have been

Figure 5. The percent of MPs aged 40 years or under in legislatures across the globe

Figure 6. The median age of MPs across the globe

any changes in the age composition of parliaments over the past decades. This dearth of knowledge of trends over time makes it difficult to say whether we could expect a change in the years to come, and if so in which direction. This section provides an overview of youth representation over time in the four selected countries of Australia, Germany, France, and the United Kingdom. We use these countries mainly because of data availability, not only on the age for all legislators going several parliaments back, but also because we can match them with available data for party delegations and cabinets in the ensuing chapters. To calculate our age statistics for the four countries going back in time, we mainly utilized web-scraped data obtained from the EveryPolitician project.

In more detail, figures 7, 8, 9, and 10 display the diachronic development of our measures of youth representation in these four countries. What comes to the fore immediately is that youths' presence has not improved over the past 20 or 30 years, regardless of how we measure it. If at all, the composition in the four parliaments has gotten slightly older, since the mean and median age increased from slightly under 50 years to slightly above 50 years in these parliaments over the past 40 years (see figs. 7 and 8). To illustrate, if we were to draw a trend line for both the mean and median age of legislators in each parliament, this line would be pointing slightly upwards for Australia, Germany, and the United Kingdom.

For Australia, we can also see that there is some variation between years. Most notably, the "negative" outlier is 2001 with a parliament whose average member was nearly 60 years old at the time of its constitution. All major parties were drivers of this trend, as the three main parties (the Liberal Party, the National Party, and Australian Labor Party) all had parliamentary groups that were, on average, 57 years or older. It is also interesting to note that the prior parliament was more than ten years younger, and that the same major parties occupied most seats in this parliament as well. For Germany and the United Kingdom, there is relatively little variation between the years; the mean and median age has consistently hovered around 50 years (i.e., in the 1980s, 1990s, and 2000s the age was slightly under 50 years and in the 2010s somewhat above).

For France, because of restricted data availability, we can only describe the diachronic development of the mean and median age over the past four elections. If we were to graph this development, it would follow a curvilinear relationship. The National Assembly elected in 2017 has been considerably younger than the previous ones (i.e., both the mean and median age of parliamentarians dropped by five years). The fact that President Macron

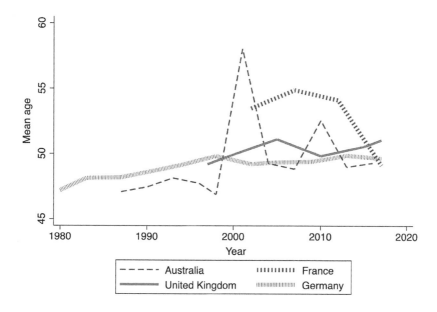

Figure 7. The mean age of MPs in Australia, France, Germany, and the United Kingdom across time

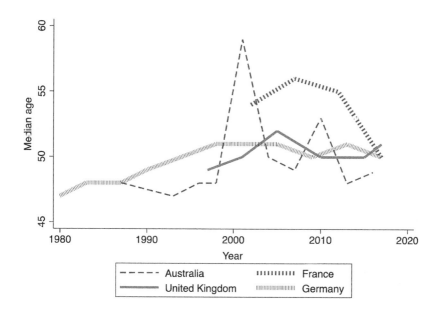

Figure 8. The median age of MPs in Australia, France, Germany, and the United Kingdom across time

formed a new political party, La République En Marche! (LREM), which was pro-European and largely appealed to younger voters, most likely allowed the party to nominate younger candidates as well. The average LREM MP was 46 years old in 2017, and more than 30 percent of legislators were under 40 years. Because En Marche! won a majority of seats, this dropped the overall age in the French National Assembly. Except for the other new party, La France Insoumise, whose average age of representatives was around 45, all other parties had MPs with an average age of around 55.

If we look at the development of the percentage of young MPs in the four countries, we get an even more complete picture of youth underrepresentation. In fact, for Australia, France, Germany, and the United Kingdom, the percentage of young legislators aged 35 years or under has hovered between 0 and 14 percent for the last three decades. The parliament with the fewest young parliamentarians was Australia in 2001 (with zero members aged 35 years or under), and the parliament with the highest number of young MPs was Macron's 2017 parliament with nearly 15 percent of the members aged 35 years or under at the beginning of the parliamentary term. Figure 9 further highlights that in most of the elections in the four countries, MPs aged 35 years or under have made up less than 10 percent of the legislators.

Figure 10, which displays the percentage of young legislators aged 40 years or under, shows that legislators up to 40 years of age make up approximately 20 percent of members in most parliaments. We also see that there is hardly any outlier with a high share of young parliamentarians aged 40 years or under (i.e., the parliament with most young members was Australia in 1987 with nearly 29 percent of MPs aged 40 years or under). Yet there are outliers with few young members up to 40 years. For example, the aforementioned Australian 2001 parliament had a mere 1.3 percent young MPs aged 40 years or under. Another downward outlier is France in 2007, with only 5.5 percent MPs aged 40 years or under. Similar to figures 7 and 10, we also find that the most variation in the percentage of young parliamentarians happens in Australia.

Even if they provide only a snapshot of youth representation across time, figures 7, 8, 9, and 10 highlight an alarming trend. Contrary to other outgroups in politics such as women, youths' presence has not increased in the previous decades. To illustrate, women's representation in national parliaments across the globe increased from 11.3 percent in 1995 to 24.3 percent as of February 2019 (UN Women 2019). Over the same period, youth representation in these same parliaments has stagnated at very low levels. Given that parliaments have not rejuvenated over the past decades, it is even more

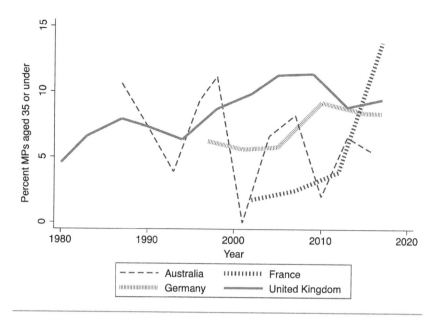

Figure 9. The percent of MPs aged 35 or under in Australia, France, Germany, and the United Kingdom across time

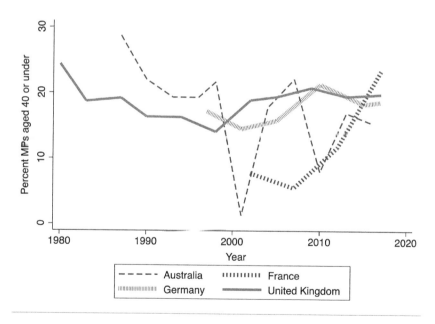

Figure 10. The percent of MPs aged 40 or under in Australia, France, Germany, and the United Kingdom across time

important that we investigate which factors render legislatures more open toward young members. Below, we discuss the country-level factors that could explain variation in the percentage of young MPs across nations.

3.3. Explanatory Factors for the Variation in Youth Representation across Countries

There is a small but growing literature that tries to determine the factors explaining variation in youth representation across countries (e.g., Joshi 2013, 2015; Stockemer and Sundström 2018; Krook and Nugent 2018). This literature mostly has an institutional emphasis, mainly focusing on youth quotas, the electoral system type, and the minimum age to run for office. We add to these institutional factors several socioeconomic and cultural indicators, such as countries' level of economic development and the median age in the population. Our goal is to get a holistic view of the factors that could explain why some parliaments have a composition of MPs that is older than others.

3.3.1. Institutional Determinants of Youth Representation

Quota Rules

The literature on youth quotas has both a normative and an empirical dimension. The more normative strand of this literature discusses why or why not countries and parties should adopt quota policies and reservation schemes for youth (see Tremmel et al. 2015; Trantidis 2016). For example, the literature advances that such proactive measures could have two advantages: they control for descriptive inequalities in the representative system (see Dahlerup 2007) and they provide a means for more intergenerational justice. Kaloianov (2015, 9–10) proposes such a generational justice argument and sees quota rules or reservation schemes for youth in the light of their political marginalization: "Quotas for the disadvantaged remove those hindrances [of performance of those affected] and improve the justice of treatment and recruitment of members of discriminated-against social groups." Yet others, such as Bidadanure (2015a), are hesitant to embrace such a generational argument, because young individuals do not face unequal treatment throughout their life. When they get older, they too will benefit from policies geared toward the elderly. Therefore Bidadanure (2015b) adheres to the view that youths' absence in positions of political power is likely a function of their lack of experience rather than a sign of discrimination. In her view, the argument to support youth quotas should be instrumental rather than intrinsic, focusing on the difference that youth might make once elected.

As for gender quotas, we can differentiate between three types of youth quotas (see Krook 2007, 2010): 1) reservation schemes, 2) legislative party clauses, and 3) voluntary party quotas.[2] Empirically, youth quotas are the exception rather than the rule. Less than ten countries have any binding quota provision for the country's lower house (see table 4).[3] Closely following our definitions, these quotas generally set the benchmark at 30, 35, or 40 years of age. Yet these mandatory quota rules frequently have a very low threshold, setting the quota bar for parliamentary representation of the young between 3 and 15 percent (IPU 2018, 2021). In early 2020, when we asked the IPU for an updated list of youth quotas, which we received per email, we got the following information. Kenya reserves 3.4 percent of its seats to youth under 35 years. Uganda's reserves 1.3 percent of seats for young adults under the age of 30. Others use legislative quotas (i.e., Rwanda, at 7.7 percent, and Morocco, at 7.6 percent). To our knowledge, Kyrgyzstan has the most ambitious legislative youth quota: it amounts to 15 percent of seats. Other countries combine quotas for youth and other minorities such as women (e.g., the Philippines) or apply them to certain districts only (e.g., Tunisia) (see also IPU 2018).[4] The IPU lists another 15 countries where at least one parliamentary party has some type of youth quotas. Yet these quotas do not necessarily apply to the lower house. For example, in Mexico the Partido Revolucionario Institucional has a youth quota, which only refers to seats in the Senate. In addition, the quota threshold and the mechanisms

---

2. Reservation schemes are binding quota rules; they reserve a certain number or percentage of parliamentary seats for the young. Legislative party clauses are binding as well. They are national legislation requiring parties to include a certain number or percentage of young people in the pool of candidates. In proportional representation systems, they can also determine where on the list parties must nominate young people. Finally, parties can decide to adopt voluntary party quotas. These measures are entirely discretionary; each party can determine the threshold and implementation.

3. In several of these countries, there are also youth quotas in place with a gender component. In some settings, such as the electoral law in Mexico, gender parity among all candidates is required. Other settings, such as the parliament of Rwanda, require gender parity among elected MPs in the assembly. Further, in settings such as the Philippines and Nicaragua there are combinations of a single quota policy targeting both women and young candidates simultaneously (see IPU 2018).

4. In Tunisia, in every district with four or more members at least one young candidate should be placed in one of the top four positions.

Table 4. Youth reservation and quota schemes in legislatures across the globe[1]

Reservations	Legislated party quota	Voluntary party quota
Kenya	Egypt	Angola
Morocco	Gabon	Croatia
Rwanda	Kyrgyzstan	Cyprus
Uganda	Philippines	El Salvador
	Tunisia	Hungary
		Lithuania
		Mexico
		Montenegro
		Mozambique
		Nicaragua
		Romania
		Senegal
		Sweden
		Turkey
		Ukraine
		Vietnam

1. In addition, Peru, Sri Lanka, Timor-Leste, Tunisia, and Uganda have implemented some type of youth quota at the local level. Kenya also has youth quotas for the upper house (see IPU 2018). Sweden is an unclear case: although IPU suggests that the party has a youth quota, we found that this is rather a guideline taken by members.

for implementation for these party quotas listed on the IPU website are not always clear.[5] Because few countries and parties have adopted age quotas and because the quota provision is under 10 percent in most cases (Kyrgyzstan would be a rare case, where it is 15 percent), we expect that quotas should only play a limited role in accounting for variation in youth representation across countries.

Electoral Systems

For the second variable, the electoral system type, we expect that compared to majoritarian systems, proportional representation (PR) systems should decrease the age of members elected to parliament. At least in theory, PR systems are likely to foster a diversification of the pool of those elected to office. We can think of four reasons why PR should be beneficial to youth. First, single-member majoritarian systems create a zero-sum game for par-

5. Legislative documents rarely mention voluntary party quotas, making the collection of information about these types of affirmative action difficult. Moreover, since some smaller parties might have informal rules, or formal yet not widely known ones, it is possible that the list of countries with voluntary party quotas is not complete (see IPU 2018).

ties, and each district is like a separate election. In order to win, every party faces strong incentives to put forward the candidate that, on average, can garner the most votes. In most districts, middle-aged to senior men of the dominant ethnicity with high education fulfill this profile best (Henig and Henig 2001). In such a system, young candidates are suboptimal: they are not as attractive to the large majority of voters, they do not have the connections necessary for valuable fundraising, and they frequently do not have the electoral capital to win the nomination. In contrast, the same zero-sum mentality does not exist in PR systems, as parties have an incentive to diversify their slates to appeal to as many constituencies as possible; this includes the young (see Matland 2005).

Second, PR systems are party-centered. This means that party elites can push forward certain types of candidates such as the young (Norris 2006). In contrast, majoritarian systems are candidate-centered. Such systems disfavor young candidates. Third, the mechanical effects of PR and plurality are different. PR normally tends to generate multiparty systems, whereas plurality favors two-party systems. Multiparty systems could indirectly benefit young individuals (Joshi 2013), because the barriers to gain representation are lower. This means that progressive parties could gain sizeable representation (an example would be the green parties in Germany and the Nordic countries). In terms of political appeal, these parties are not only popular among young voters but might also represent a new generation of representatives: MPs that are younger, less traditional, and more geared toward issues interesting to young voters, such as the abolishment of the draft or fostering policies geared toward the protection of the environment (Siaroff 2000).

Fourth, PR systems are more prone to a contagion effect; that is, if one party starts to nominate greater numbers of young candidates, other parties are likely to follow suit. More generally, under PR a party can likely respond positively to calls to nominate young contestants in greater numbers (Fawcett 2018). For one, it does not have to convince incumbents or other senior party members to step aside, as there might still be space on the party list to nominate young politicians as well (Joshi 2013). In addition, the gains for diversifying the electoral slate might be larger under PR. Adding just a few young candidates to the list could give the party a younger and more dynamic output. The same would not necessarily happen in first-past-the-post systems, even if a party was to nominate several young candidates, because these candidates would only be visible in the districts they run, rather than nationally or regionally (Matland and Studlar 1996).

The Minimum Age to Stand for Office

As a third institutional factor, we hypothesize that the minimum age candidates must have to stand for office should influence the composition of parliaments. While the voting age is 18 years in most countries in our sample, the legal candidacy age requirements differ more in some countries, from 18 years for countries like Austria and Germany to 35 years for Tajikistan. It is likely that formal age limits at 25, 30, or 35 years will hinder young politicians' access to parliament both directly and indirectly—directly since such rules hinder the youngest candidates from running and indirectly since it sends the signal to potential candidates that politics is not a business for young people (UNDP 2013). In addition, having different age requirements for voting and for running for office might send the message to young individuals that politics is not their domain; being only allowed to vote but not to stand for elected office implies that they are not full political citizens yet (IPU 2014, 2021). There is also growing empirical evidence that having lower age barriers to stand for office benefits the presence of the young. For example, both Stockemer and Sundström (2018) and Krook and Nugent's (2018) large N analyses confirm that countries with low age barriers to run for office (e.g., 18 years) tend to have a higher share of young MPs than countries with candidacy requirements with a higher age bar (e.g., 25 or 30 years).

3.3.2. Socioeconomic and Cultural Determinants of Youth Representation

Median Age in the Voting-Age Population

In theory, the age distribution within the voting-age population may be an important predictor of the share of young legislators in parliament. If voters are seeking representatives that reflect their own interests, they may choose candidates that are roughly their age (Henn and Foard 2012). For the individual level, this would imply that adults in their 20s and 30s should be more inclined to vote for candidates who are roughly their age. They can do so by either selecting certain candidates or by supporting parties with more young candidates on their party lists. For the macro-level, this would then entail that voting-age populations with a younger citizenry should have parliaments with a larger share of youths, on average.

However, in practice we are skeptical that the voting-age population plays a large role in lowering the median and mean age of legislators, or in increasing the share of young MPs. In democracies, as well as electoral autocracies, the idea that young citizens are likely to vote for young representatives relies on the precondition that they actually find young candidates for whom they can vote. In many settings, this might not be the case, as parties might not put forward (enough) young candidates. And if parties put them forward, these young candidates might find themselves on noneligible list positions or in districts where they have little chance of winning. A quick look at the empirical data in our sample supports this more pessimistic view. There are many examples with very young populations and very old parliaments. One of the prime examples would be Angola. The median age in the population of this African country is slightly under 17 years; yet the median age of Angola's parliamentarians is 63.5 years old. Even if the age difference is not as flagrant as in Angola, Senegal is another example of a "grey" parliament and a young citizenry (i.e., the median age of parliamentarians is 57, whereas the median Senegalese citizen is only 19 years old).

Development

According to the influential postmaterialism thesis, changing values in the citizenry should accompany economic development. In particular, the transformation from industrial to postindustrial or service sector societies should trigger a change in dominant values. While in agrarian societies— and, to a lesser degree, industrial ones—traditional and materialist values ought to prevail, service sector societies should be characterized by postmaterialist values, where people are more likely to favor gender equality, environmental protection, and participation in decision-making (Inglehart and Norris 2003). This postmaterialist shift has been argued to result in a higher demand for having newcomers in elected office and could therefore be beneficial to the representation of out-groups such as ethnic minorities and women (Stockemer 2015).

Hypothetically, and at first glance, the same should apply to youth. Young citizens often believe in progressive values. Be it in the fight against climate change, the drive for equality of the sexes, or for a more participatory democracy, it is mainly young adults in their 20s and 30s that push these issues (Janmaat and Keating 2019). From this argument, we can deduce that young citizens should also be beneficiaries of a postmaterialist environment and possibly gain higher presence in politics. Yet, at second glance, the idea that the postmaterialist shift has triggered highly interested and politically engaged youth does not seem to be true. As we have shown in chapter 2, youth today show low levels of conventional political participation and face a cycle of political alienation. It is true that some parliaments have become more open to out-groups, such as women and ethnic minority groups. The same does not seem to be the case for the group of young adults; it seems that parliaments have remained resistant to these trends of renewal and change.

In many respects, parliaments have adopted to the requirements of the 21st century. They have an online presence and carry other attributes of being modern organizations. Nevertheless, they are generally still, as our data strongly suggest, traditional institutions, mostly dominated by the older cohorts of the population; this finding applies regardless of whether we look at postmaterialist or traditional countries. Hence we expect economic development—which is the main operationalization of the value change thesis in the literature—to play a small role in explaining variation in youth representation across the globe.

Corruption

There are several theoretical reasons why young candidates may face obstacles to gain election in highly corrupt contexts. Besides formal political institutions, there are also informal procedures that might influence the representation of various groups in parliament. One of these informal aspects might be levels of corruption, which can affect the processes of recruitment in politics, since it "indicates the presence of 'shadowy arrangements' that benefit the already privileged" (Sundström and Wängnerud 2016, 355). Rather than the young, these privileged are likely to be senior individuals, who are often the agents of networks of the privileged in corrupt contexts. In Bjarnegård's words (2013, 37), the existence of corruption or clientelism should benefit candidates that are within the dominant norm:

> Only those with access to networks, those with connections within the local or national elite, those with resources to finance corrupt behavior, and those who are already influential in society are in positions to be considered assets in clientelist networks and are the only ones who will be trusted with the sensitive nature of the exchange.

For these theoretical reasons, we could infer that the middle-aged and older generations are overrepresented in parliaments of countries where corruption is widespread. Nevertheless, the empirical record of countries with low levels of corruption concerning youth representation does not look as rosy as theory predicts. We note that some frontrunners in the fight against corruption (i.e., nations that tend to rank the highest in cross-country measures of corruption), such as Sweden, also have high shares of young MPs. (i.e., this Nordic country has nearly 24 percent young parliamentarians aged 35 years or under, and 37 percent MPs aged 40 years or under). Yet other countries in the group of the ten least corrupt countries in the world, such as Luxembourg, have rather old parliaments. (i.e., the median age of parliamentarians in this Benelux country is 54.5 years, and the share of young legislators (those aged 35 years or under) hovers around 10 percent, which is only average). On the other hand, not all highly corrupt countries have low shares of young legislators. For example, the three countries with the highest share of young parliamentarians aged 35 years or under (i.e., Armenia, Serbia, and Kosovo) are all ranked below average in their corruption rating. Given these empirical discrepancies, we only expect a weak, if any, relationship between low corruption scores and high shares of young MPs.

Share of Muslims in the Population

A traditional lifestyle, patriarchy, and hierarchical power structures characterize Islam as a religion, in particular in its traditional form (see Weiffen 2004). Blaydes and Linzer (2008) show that a strict and traditional interpretation of Islam prevents out-groups, such as women and religious minorities, from advancing in politics. Norris's finding (1999) bolsters this claim; she indicates that societies with a high share of Muslims in the population tend to have a poor record of including women in their legislatures. We believe that the political elite in Muslim-dominant countries may also be reluctant to welcome young cohorts in their parliaments. This should be the case, because seniority is frequently a primary factor for recruitment to elite positions in such contexts.

Nevertheless, the empirical record of Muslim-majority countries and non-Muslim majority countries might not be as clear as theory predicts. For example, three Muslim-majority countries (Yemen, Uzbekistan, and Kosovo) are among the few countries with 30 percent or more young legislators aged 40 years or under. In contrast, some of the countries with very few Muslims in their population have zero members of parliament aged 40 years or under, including Monaco, Jamaica, and Palau. Hence, again, the relationship seems to be less clear than the literature suggests.

Regime Type

In theory, a democratic state should give all adult citizens equal opportunities to participate in the political life; alongside individuals of all genders, backgrounds, and religions, this should also include the young. Therefore, compared to autocracies, we could expect countries with democratic rule to have a higher likelihood to include people from a diverse set of groups. While theoretically there should be a clear link between the democratic ideal and increased representation of all groups in society, the actual relationship between regime types and other traditional out-groups questions this ideal (see Paxton et al. 2010). For youth, there is only some preliminary evidence from Russia illustrating that youth could benefit from a democratic system of government (i.e., the article by Golosov [2014] reports that with the country's path toward greater authoritarianism, young individuals' access to regional parliaments has decreased over several election cycles in the 2000s). Yet the empirical record of other democracies renders the possibility of a generalization beyond Russia unlikely, to say the least. For example, we do not find a decrease in the age of parliamentarians over time in the four democracies that we cover in this chapter. More generally, some of the longest-lived democracies, for instance the United States, have some of the legislatures with the oldest composition when it comes to the age of parliamentarians. In addition, among the ten countries with the lowest median age of parliament, there are only four democracies (i.e., the two consolidated democracies San Marino and Andorra and the two fledgling democracies Armenia and Kosovo). On the other hand, two of the three "oldest" parliaments are in fact democracies (i.e., Jamaica and Palau). Nevertheless, we include democracy as an additional independent variable and gauge whether this system of government has any influence on youth representation in our analysis.

3.4. Research Design

To test which factors explain variation in our four measures of youth representation, we present the results of five multiple regression models, which include 129 observations.[6] On the left-hand side of each model are the four

---

6. We had to exclude San Marino and Saint Lucia from the multiple regression models because of data unavailability for one of the independent variables, countries' corruption score.

dependent variables, the median age in parliament, the mean age in parliament, the percentage of representatives aged 35 years or under, and the percentage of MPs aged 40 years or under. On the right-hand side are the proxies of our independent variables, which we describe below.

To measure our first independent variable, youth quotas, we create two variables: *Legislative age quotas,* coded 1 if there are nationally binding quotas (both reservation seats and legislative binding quotas) and *Party age quotas,* a dummy coded 1 if there is at least one party in a country with voluntary quota provisions. The reference category for both variables is the condition with no such youth quotas. The source for these variables is primarily the IPU report from 2018, as well as data we received from the IPU by email.[7] The operationalization of the second variable, different electoral system types, translates into two dummy variables, coded 1 for *Proportional Representation* (PR) and *Mixed systems,* respectively. The reference category are plurality systems (IPU 2019). Our third variable, *Minimum age to stand for election,* measures the age of eligibility in years to become a member of the national parliament (lower house election where applicable). We also base this variable on information outlined by IPU (2019).

We construct the fourth variable, *Median age in the population,* using figures on years from the CIA World Factbook (2019a). We then gauge economic development in a country by employing the proxy measure of *Log GDP per capita* (see United Nations 2019). Our measure *Corruption* is the national indicator "control of corruption" from the World Bank's (2019) Worldwide Governance Indicators. This indicator ranges from approximately -2.5 (weak control of corruption) to 2.5 (strong control). The variable *Percentage Muslims* captures this group's share of the total population in a country. The data stems from the CIA World Factbook (2019b). Finally, our indicator of regime types is a dichotomous measure of *Democracy,* coded 1 for democracies and 0 for nondemocracies (i.e., hybrid regimes and autocracies). To assign countries in any of the two categories, we followed the recommendation of Polity IV and coded a country if it has a Polity ranking of 6 or higher (on a 10 to 10 scale) (Marshall et al. 2011). For all these variables, we match the year of these indicators with those of the election in question.

As a modeling technique, we use ordinary least squares (OLS) regres-

---

7. Unfortunately, the IPU 2018 report is not always clear on whether a country has a quota and what the quota threshold is. To further decipher the existence of a quota, we looked at the raw questionnaire that the IPU collected and that we received from the IPU. We further conducted our own Google search for each quota rule to verify or falsify the information that we obtained from the IPU.

sion with Huber White Standard Errors (see White 1980). The choice to use OLS is justified by the fact that the distribution of the dependent variables comes close to a normal distribution (see fig. 3). We add robust standard errors, because the variance across countries differs tremendously. For the third equation, the model measuring the percentage of young legislators aged 35 years or under, we present an additional equation—a Tobit model alongside an OLS model (see model 3a). The fact that this variable has a distribution that is skewed to the left and does not have a normally distributed curve justifies this choice.

3.5. Results

Our multiple regression models bring two factors to the fore that have an impact on age representation (see table 5). First, it is the institutional factor for the minimum age to stand for office, which is statistically significant and in the expected direction in all five models. On average, countries where citizens can stand for office at 18 have younger parliaments and more young MPs than countries with higher age limits. In more detail, models 1 and 2 predict that the mean and median age increases by half a year for every year we increase the eligibility requirement above 18. For example, this implies that we can predict parliaments with a legal age to run set at 30 years of age to be six years older, on average, compared to parliaments with a minimum age to stand for office at 18 years of age. Models 3 and 4 further predict that with every year the age requirements increase, the share of young parliamentarians aged 35 or 40 years or under decrease by between half a percentage point and one percentage point, respectively.

The second variable that turns out to be significant is the electoral system type in the form of proportional representation (PR). From models 1 to 4, it appears that PR matters for increasing the share of young legislators aged 35 years or under, as well as aged 40 years or under. In fact, models 3 and 4 predict that the share of young legislators increases by four and seven percentage points, respectively (i.e., four percentage points for the share of young MPs aged 35 years or under, and seven percentage points for the share of young legislators aged 40 years or under). Compared to the reference category of plurality systems, mixed systems also seem to increase the share of young parliamentarians moderately. In contrast, the electoral system does not play a role in determining the mean and median age of the composition in a parliament.

Table 5. Multiple regression models measuring the effect of national-level factors on youth representation in parliaments

	Model 1 (Mean age)	Model 2 (Median age)	Model 3 (35 or under)	Model 3a (35 or under)	Model 4 (40 or under)
Legislative age	.158	−.091	−.159	.341	.584
quotas	(1.50)	(1.69)	(1.93)	(2.94)	(3.43)
Party age quotas	1.34	1.88	.291	.305	−.100
	(1.64)	(1.62)	(2.12)	(2.25)	(3.30)
PR	−1.09	−.924	.3.49**	4.07**	5.82**
	(1.12)	(1.18)	(1.37)	(1.69)	(2.33)
Mixed	−2.11	−2.67*	3.92	4.29*	7.22*
	(1.48)	(1.47)	(2.50)	(2.21)	(4.04)
Minimum age to	.511***	.498***	−.484**	−.489**	−.980***
stand for office	(.143)	(.146)	(.223)	(.216)	(.342)
Median age in the	−.077	−.067	.125	.002	.169
population	(.070)	(.074)	(.107)	(.001)	(.168)
Log GDP per	.432*	.489*	−.503	−.521	−1.17**
capita	(258)	(.274)	(.446)	(.576)	(.570)
Corruption	−.105	.005	−.006	.027	.270
	(.574)	(.598)	(.995)	(1.04)	(1.45)
Percent Muslims in a	−.018	−.009	.001	.006	.025
country	(.018)	(.018)	(.024)	(.022)	(.039)
Democracy	.570	.318	−1.45	−2.07	−2.20
	(1.21)	(1.23)	(1.73)	(1.64)	(2.63)
Constant	38.96***	38.45***	18.82***	17.38**	42.96***
	(4.47)	(4.51)	(5.95)	(.070)	(9.65)
Rsquared	.18	.17	.15		.17
Log Likelihood				−403.04	
Root MSE	4.56	4.79	6.85		11.03
N	129	129	129	129	129

Standard errors in parentheses, *p < .10, **p < .05, ***p < .01 (two tailed).

All other variables influence neither the median age nor the mean age of legislators, nor the percentage of young legislators. The five models also have relatively poor model fit, explaining between 15 and 20 percent of the variance in the age structure of parliaments. This also implies that we can explain and predict the age composition of parliaments much less exactly than the presence of other politically marginalized groups in national parliaments, such as women, which often have a model fit of more than 50 percent (e.g., Caul 2001; Ruedin 2012). It also entails that we need further studies, with more fine-grained predictors to study variation in youth representation.

3.6. Discussion

The results obtained from this study highlight two factors: candidate age requirements to run for office and the electoral system type. As such, we confirm Stockemer and Sundström's (2018) as well as Krook and Nugent's (2018) assessment about eligibility requirements. We think that there is some robust evidence now that laws that require candidates to be 25, 30, or 35 years of age clearly hinder youths' presence in elected assemblies. These laws likely affect the election of youth directly, because they prevent young adults from running for office. They also function as a hurdle to youth indirectly, because they portray that politics is no arena for young adults. While we did not control for the voting age in our analyses—because in many of the countries we include voting rights coincide with the right to run—prior research suggests that decreasing the voting age to 18 years (where it is still 21), or possibly 16, can have a similar positive influence on youth representation. For example, in Norway, the government decided in 2011 to have 20 municipalities (about 5 percent of the total number of municipalities) undergo a reform in allowing those citizens turning 16 and 17 years during the election to vote. Both compared to other municipalities and prior election years, municipalities with a voting age of 16 elected younger local parliaments (Government of Norway 2011; Bergh 2014).

The second institutional factor to increase the share of young adults (but not the median and mean age in parliament) is proportional representation (as well as mixed electoral systems). This finding not only aligns with prior research on youth representation (see Joshi 2013, 2015), it also adds to the broader representation literature, which finds PR systems to be more favorable to politically marginalized groups than other institutionalized rules. PR systems not only increase the percentage of women in parliament, including minority women (see Hughes 2016), but also that of young adults. Hence this study adds to the voices that see proportional representation as more inclusive to out-groups (at least when these out-groups are spread rather evenly throughout the country, which is mainly the case for youth in most countries) (see Bogaards 2013).

Even if we find that age quota rules (whatever their type) do not increase youth representation, we see tremendous potential in these measures of affirmative action. As of now, youth quotas are not effective in their design. So far, they exist in only a few countries nationally, and where they do exist they sometimes lack full implementation. The prime example is Tunisia; officially, the constitution of this country stipulates that youth aged 35 years or under must make up 25 percent of the candidates. Yet in the parliament elected in 2015, they only made up 8 percent of the parliamentarians. Trying to explain this difference, Belschner (2021) concludes that the adoption of youth quotas in Tunisia was largely a case of window-dressing to curb future protests. It was a means to co-opt youth into the traditional power structures, but not an effort of real reform (see also Van Gyampo [2015] for a similar argument).

However, we believe that quota rules do have potential. For example, a 25 or 30 percent legislative quota rule for youth under 35 years for eligible seats could have a tremendous influence on youth representation. While still falling short of parity in representation between society and parliaments in many countries—especially low-income ones—such a quota could double, triple, or quadruple youth representation in many settings. In addition, such a proactive measure would send a "real" signal to youth that they have a place in politics as well. Experience with the adoption of quota provisions for other out-groups supports such conclusions. For example, while women's representation has grown steadily through incremental steps in some older democracies, quota schemes have provided significant improvements for women's presence in countries across the globe, and particularly in countries of the Global South. Examples of developing countries that benefited from a strong boost in women's representation are Rwanda and Mozambique (Tripp and Kang 2008). Youth representation could undergo a similar development if countries decided to be proactive and allow youth a certain presence. Unfortunately, it does not seem that the political will is there for such a move. Yet age-based quotas are probably the only fast-track measure to align youth representation in politics with their representation in society.

Implementing quota rules is not the only measure countries could adopt to increase youth representation. In theory, non-PR systems could switch to PR. However, due to the multidimensionality of effects and the stickiness of electoral rules, changing the electoral system is complex in practice and is likely to face opposition by vested interests. Yet what is comparatively easy is changing the legal age barriers to stand for office, particularly in those countries where there is a mismatch between the right to run for office and the right to stand for office. We also believe that from a normative perspective it is questionable, to say the least, to grant young adults partial citizenship rights. How can we justify that the age of majority demands potential duties of individuals—such as military conscription or paying taxes—and grants some rights, such as those to drive, buy alcohol, or to vote, but still not others, such as the possibility for adults to stand for office? For us, having full citizenship rights should also involve the possibility to effectively partake in decision-making and we think society should grant this right at the same time as any other citizenship rights. The proposal to reform such rules is also relatively easy to implement. However, such reforms are naturally contingent on the political will to take the required action, which seems to be still lacking in jurisdictions with age requirements to stand for office set at 25 or 30.

CHAPTER 4

YOUTH REPRESENTATION ACROSS PARTY DELEGATIONS IN PARLIAMENT

> The narrow social composition of legislatures suggests either that certain groups within society are less capable of representing others, or that something has gone awry in the recruitment process
>
> (MURRAY 2014, P. 520)

4.1. Youths' (under) Representation across Party Delegations

Party organizations shape the opportunities for young aspiring politicians to reach political office; they decide whom to recruit and promote, as well as how much support to give to candidates (see Kittilson 2006; Bjarnegård 2013). Therefore youths' presence in national assemblies should not only be a feature of national factors (i.e., candidate age requirements and electoral system type) but also a function of intraparty candidate selection processes (Sanbonmatsu 2002). Therefore it is important to get a better understanding of the party level factors that explain patterns of youth representation in parliamentary party groups. We engage in this type of analysis across the highest possible number of parliamentary delegations (270 parties across 52 countries, referring to the lower house when a country has a bicameral legislature). Before doing so, we present some univariate statistics on the distribution of elected young adults across our sample of party groups.

As a data source, we again use the website EveryPolitician (2019). We calculate our four age measures at the start of each parliamentary term. The election years we cover range from 2012 to 2019. Unfortunately, we could not collect party data for all 131 countries because of incomplete country data for some countries or the lack of party affiliation data for other countries on the EveryPolitician website. Data availability for the variable party ideology also restricted the number of parties we could include. Our sample is therefore limited to mainly OECD countries, but it also includes other countries from various parts of the world (including India and South

Africa).[1] For the 52 countries for which we could retrieve data, we tried to be as inclusive as possible, collecting data for all parties with at least seven members in parliament. We chose seven elected members as a cut-off point for several reasons. First, there must be a minimum number of members in a parliamentary group to compute our dependent variables, the median and mean party age, and the percentage of young legislators aged 35 and 40 years or under. Second, the Westminster system requires parties to have a certain number of deputies to gain certain parliamentary rights, including staff and office space. For example, in Canada this number is 12. We have deliberately chosen a threshold below this number to be as inclusive as possible. Third, most countries with a legislative threshold set this metric between 3 and 5 percent of the vote, and we want to have comparable parties in countries with no electoral threshold. We use Belgium as a benchmark. This Benelux country has a comparatively small parliament and a high threshold. To illustrate, since 2003 Belgium has had a 150-person assembly and an electoral threshold of 5 percent. This roughly translates into seven seats required to be represented in the Belgian parliament (Hooghe and Deschower 2011). In other countries, the cutoff point of seven members includes parties with a lower share than 5 percent. For example, the Swedish Miljöpartiet just made the cut to enter parliament, with roughly 4 percent of the votes in the 2018 elections, and sent 16 MPs to parliament. Our cutoff point of seven MPs guarantees that we have comparable parties in our dataset.

In our sample of 270 party delegations, the mean and median age at the start of each parliament is roughly 49.0 years old. The percentage of young MPs aged 35 years or under is 12.3 percent. The share of young legislators aged 40 years or under is 24.2 percent at the beginning of each parliamentary term (see fig. 11). This implies that the share of young adults is slightly higher in our sample of party delegations in comparison to our larger sample of legislatures in the previous chapter. There is also wide variation in the percentage of young adults that different parties send to the national legislature. The mean and median age across party delegations in our sample ranges from roughly 33 years to about 63. The youngest party delegation is the one of the Five Star Movement in Italy, elected in 2013 (Movimento

---

1. Our dataset on parties includes parties in the following 52 countries: Armenia, Australia, Austria, Azerbaijan, Belgium, Bulgaria, Canada, Croatia, Cyprus, Czech Republic, Denmark, Estonia, Finland, France, Georgia, Germany, Greece, Hungary, Iceland, India, Ireland, Israel, Italy, Japan, Latvia, Lithuania, Luxembourg, Malta, Mexico, Moldova, Montenegro, the Netherlands, New Zealand, North Macedonia, Norway, Poland, Portugal, Romania, Russia, Serbia, Slovakia, Slovenia, South Africa, South Korea, Spain, Sri Lanka, Sweden, Switzerland, Taiwan, Turkey, the United Kingdom, and the United States.

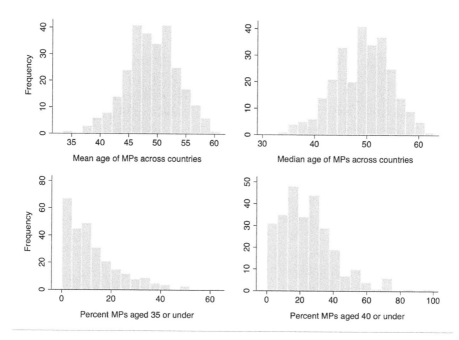

Figure 11. The age distribution of MPs across party delegations in 52 countries in or around 2019

Cinque Stelle [M5S]). At the time of this election, the party's delegation was roughly 33.4 years old. Among the ten youngest delegations are all sorts of parties, such as radical right-wing parties (e.g., The Movement for a Better Hungary, better known under the name of Jobbik) and green parties in Sweden and Belgium, as well as more traditional parties, such as the Peoples' Party in Slovakia.

The oldest delegation belongs to the Communist Party in Moldova, with a median age of 63 years at the time of the election in 2014. In fact, there seems to be a trend that communist party representatives in parliament are among the oldest, given that among the ten oldest parties are three communist parties (the Communist Party of the Russian Federation and the French Communist Party alongside the aforementioned Moldovan party). Interestingly, the two main parties in the US, the Democratic Party and the Republican Party are also among the ten oldest delegations in our sample, with a median age of roughly 60 and 58 years, respectively, in the 116th House of Representatives (taking office in 2019).

If we look at the party delegations with the highest share of parliamentarians aged 35 years or under, we have four parties whose share of MPs in this age span are 50 percent or higher. In addition to the Five Star Movement, these parties are the Save Romania Union, the Green Party in Sweden and the Socialist Party in the Netherlands. On the other side of the coin, there are 49 out of the 270 party delegations that did not send any single legislator 35 years or under to parliament. The list includes some well-known parties such as the Socialist Party in France, Labour in Ireland, and the Slovenian Democratic Party. When it comes to parties with delegations with a majority of legislators aged 40 years or under, we have 23 parties in our sample. Most of these parties are small, including the Red-Green Alliance in Denmark and the New Flemish Alliance in Belgium. In contrast, there are also 21 parties without a single MP aged 40 years or under. While this list includes many small parties as well, it also includes some more well-known parties, such as the Centre Party in Iceland, which won nearly 11 percent of the vote in 2017 or the AKEL—Left—New Forces in Cyprus, which won nearly 26 percent of the vote in 2016.

What is evident in our party data is that there is substantial variation between parties in the share of young adults they send to their national parliament. Later in this chapter, we investigate this variation, but before doing so we look at the evolution of youth representation over time in selected party delegations in the parliaments of Australia, France, Germany, and the United Kingdom.

4.2. Young Adults in Australian, German, French, and British Party Delegations over Time

To show how youths' presence has developed over time across party groups of MPs, we look at delegations of the major parties in Australia, France, Germany, and the United Kingdom. For each country, we display the temporal development of the median age and the percentage of MPs aged 40 or under. We only display these two indicators because the party data on mean age largely mimics the data on the median age. For the percentage of young legislators aged 35 years or under, the overall proportion of young parliamentarians is too small for most years to account for meaningful variation over time.

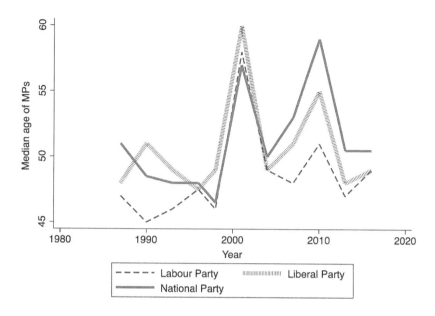

Figure 12. The median age of MPs in the main Australian party delegations to parliament across time

Australia

For the first country, Australia, we can see that the median age of parliamentarians has developed very similarly across the three main parties, the Australian Labor Party, the Liberal Party of Australia and the National Party of Australia (see fig. 12). A predominance of relatively old MPs characterizes all three party delegations, with a median age over 50 years for most parliaments. The 2001 and 2010 elections also triggered a particularly old legislature, with all parties electing older politicians compared to the election before. Because the three parties' curves follow each other so closely, there seems to be also some kind of contagion effect. It appears that if one of the parties decided to nominate younger representatives, as in 1998, the other parties would follow suit. Conversely, if one party decided to nominate older members, our data suggests that other parties would act in a similar way. This also implies that in Australia, unlike in other countries—Germany in particular, as discussed below—there has been little variation in youth representation across parties.

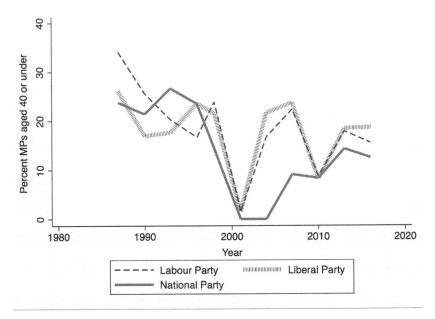

Figure 13. The percent of MPs aged 40 years or under in the main Australian party delegations across time

Figure 13 confirms the idea that youth representation develops in waves. This becomes particularly visible if we look at the 2001 election where the group of MPs aged 40 years or under were literally absent across all parties. In contrast, in the prior election, which triggered the youngest parliament over the past three decades, the delegations of Labour, the Liberal Party, and the National Party all consisted of between 15 and 25 percent young adults (aged 40 years or under). More broadly, figure 12 reveals an alarming trend: the percentage of young parliamentarians has decreased, rather than increased, over the years. To illustrate, all three parties had a higher share of young legislators in 1987 than in 2018. Overall, this indicates that youth have not gained traction in the three major party delegations in Australia over the past 30 years.

France

Turning our attention to France, unfortunately, we have less data, covering only four elections. This renders it harder to come up with a solid assess-

Table 6. Development of the median age and the share of MPs aged 40 or under in French party delegations

Year	The Republicans / UMP	Socialist Party	MoDem / UDF	Communist Party	LREM / En Marche!	Un-submissive France)	National Rally)
Median Age							
2002	54	54	51	57.5			
2007	56	56	54				
2012	56	55					
2017	53	55	58	59	50	48	48.5
Aged 40 or under							
2002	8.3	4.9	15.4	0			
2007	5.7	4.1	4.2				
2012	9.5	14.7					
2017	15.2	3.2	0	9.1	32.6	42.9	12.5

ment of youth representation across the major French party delegations over time. Nevertheless, table 6 illustrates some fairly clear tendencies: the parliamentarians of the established parties are generally rather old. In detail, the median age has been over 50 years for all elections between 2002 and 2017 for the three major parties—The Republicans (formerly named the Union for a Popular Movement [UMP]), the Democratic Movement, (MoDem—previously organized as the Union for French Democracy [UDF]), and the Socialist Party. The main parties have also sent very few members aged 40 years or under to the National Assembly. Over the course of the four elections, the delegations of the Republicans, the Socialist Party, and the MoDem never had more than 15 percent young MPs. The French example also confirms the old age of members of communist organizations. The median age of the delegation of the French Communist Party was 57.5 years in 2002 and 59 in 2017. The communists also did not reach 10 percent of young legislators aged 40 years or under in the two elections in which they put seven or more members in the National Assembly.

The situation for young politicians in the new parties looks somewhat brighter. Macron's party, LREM, which won a landslide in 2017, sent a delegation to parliament with a median age of 50 and a mean age of 46 years. The party also had more than 30 percent of its MPs aged 40 or under at the time of the election. With a median age of 48, the other new party, La France Insoumise (or Un-submissive France), which Jean-Luc Mélenchon founded just months before the election, also sent a somewhat younger delegation to the French National Assembly. At the inauguration of the 2017 parliament, the party had more than 40 percent of MPs aged 40 years or under. Finally, the National Rally (previously National Front), who sent eight members to the 2017 to 2022 parliament, had a median age of 48.5 years and one member aged 40 years or under.

Germany

For the next country, Germany, we can retrace the development of youth representation for a longer period: from 1980 to 2017 (see figs. 14, 15, and footnote 35). We can see that for the main parties, the center-right party Christian Democratic Party (CDU), its Bavarian sibling the Christian Social Union (CSU), the Social Democrats, and the Free Democrats, there is relatively little variation in either the median age of parliamentarians or the share of parliamentarians aged 40 years or under over the past four decades. Over the years, the median age has vacillated around 50 years and the percentage of young legislators around 20 percent. As such, these data clearly confirm that parliaments have not gotten younger. In other words, Germany has not made significant progress in improving youth representation in the Federal Parliament.

We also see a trend that the parliamentary delegations of new parties get older, once these parties become more established. This rings true for the Green Party and the Left Party. Except for the first time it entered parliament in 1983, the Green Party had a young delegation throughout the 1980s and 1990s. However, for every legislative period thereafter, its MPs grew older and the percentage of parliamentarians aged 40 years or under decreased. The Left Party has undergone some similar developments, with younger delegations in the 1990s and older caucuses for the more recent elections.[2] Hence it seems from the German example that young parties provide an opportunity for young people to gain influence and representation. However, the more these parties mature, the more youth representation appears to decline.

---

2. We here refer to its organizational roots in the Party of Democratic Socialism (PDS), which was formed in 1990 as a successor party to the Socialist Unity Party (SED). With a merger of PDS and the Labour and Social Justice Party (WASG) in 2007, the current Left Party was established. For the figures over time, numbers before the German reunification refer to those of parties with a legislative presence in West Germany.

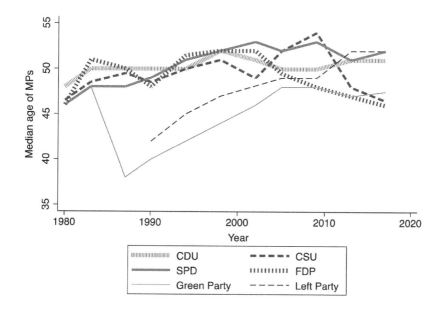

Figure 14. The median age of MPs in the main German party delegations across time

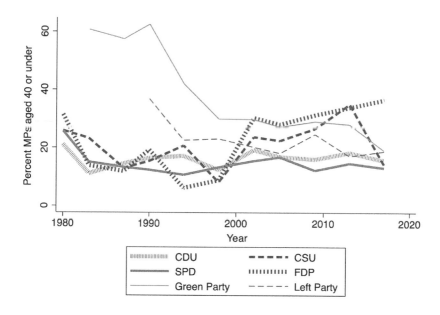

Figure 15. The percent of MPs aged 40 years or under in the main German party delegations across time

The United Kingdom

Our data on youth representation in the party delegations of the United Kingdom spans across 20 years and largely reflects the trends from the other three countries (see figs. 16 and 17). Again, figures refer to the lower house of this bicameral legislature, the House of Commons. The two major parties, the Conservative and Unionist Party (i.e., the Tories) and the Labour Party, have had a stable age structure in their delegations between 1997 and 2017. The median age for the two parties has hovered around 50 years, a little below 50 for the Conservatives and a little above for Labour. The share of legislators aged 40 years or under has been slightly lower for Labour than it has been for the Conservatives; it has floated around 20 percent for both parties. Even more interestingly, the Liberal Democrats confirm the observations from the Green Party and the Left Party in Germany; that is, when a new party becomes more established, its median age tends to increase and its share of young parliamentarians tends to decrease. Founded in 1988, the median age of this center party's representatives in Westminster has become older over time (the increase from a median age of 49 years in 1997 to 56 years in 2017 is quite considerable). Even more visible, the share of MPs aged 40 years or under within this party delegation has shrunk over time, from more than 30 percent to around 15 percent, between 1997 and 2017.

Taken together, the distributions of youth in party delegations—both across the 270 parties in our full sample and over time in the parliamentary party delegations in the four selected countries—provide some interesting results. First, we find that the age distribution in parties' parliamentary delegations differs widely, from a median of 33 years to a median of more than 63 years. Second, there is wide variation in how many young adults parties send to the national parliament as a share of their full delegation, ranging from zero to over half of all their MPs, if we take those aged 40 years or under as the benchmark. Third, there seems to be no major differences between center-right and center-left parties in their tendency to have young legislators. For most parties, the median age hovers around 50 years in their parliamentary group, while communist parties seem to be a party family with some of the oldest parliamentarians. Fourth, the temporal patterns of youths' presence appear largely unchanged over the past decades, at least for the established parties in the four Western democracies we study. In other words, youth have not gained traction in major parties. In contrast, they seem to be more highly represented in younger parties. Yet the diachronic analysis suggests that as parties become older, the average age of their rep-

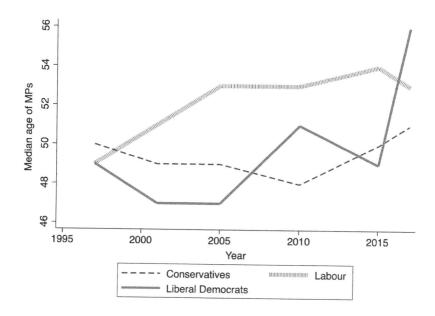

Figure 16. The median age of MPs in the main party delegations in the United Kingdom across time

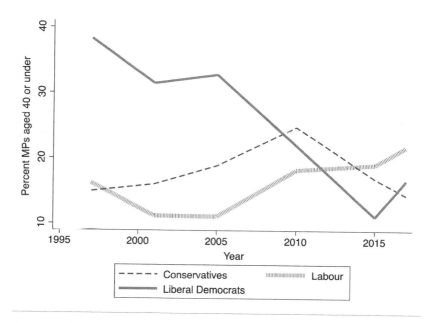

Figure 17. The percent of MPs aged 40 years or under in the main party delegations in the United Kingdom across time

resentatives increases too, both in their median and mean age. In addition, the share of young MPs declines with the maturation of parliamentary parties. This aging of party delegations happens despite some turnover in the representatives. In fact, this makes us think about Robert Michels's famous "iron law of oligarchy," which states that all parties, however progressive and participatory they are at their creation, become hierarchical structures over time (see Berger 2017). It seems that the aging of the party's representatives is a byproduct of this hierarchization. In other words, our results support the notion that the structure of new parties become just like others over time, including their age structure.

In the next section, we aim at explaining the cross-sectional variation in the age structure of parties in the multivariate realm, focusing on the sample of parties across the 52 countries. To do so, we test the influence of five possible explanatory variables (voluntary party youth quotas, the age of the party, the size of the party in terms of electoral success, the age of the party leader, and the political ideology of the party).

4.3. Explanatory Factors for the Variation in Youth Representation across Parties

Because there is hardly any prior research on youth representation across parties, we consult the literature on women's representation in parties and adapt the expectations put forward in this literature to explain the presence of young adults in parties. The women's representation literature focusing on parliamentary parties (see Childs and Webb 2012; Southwell 2014; Childs and Caul Kittilson 2016) has identified several characteristics, which, adapted to youth, could also affect the extent to which parties have younger MPs in their delegations. These are the existence of voluntary party quotas, the age of the party, the size of the party in terms of electoral success, the age of the party leader, and the political ideology of the party.

Party Quotas

The first explanatory factor we think could matter are voluntary youth quotas in parties. Similar to legislative quotas, youth quotas within political parties could matter for increased youth representation. They should have a threefold effect. First, they should directly boost youth representation in the party that has quotas for youth, given that quotas force elites to nominate a certain percentage of young adults on their lists or as candidates for seats in majoritarian contests. Second, they could have a psychological signaling effect to youth. By adopting voluntary youth quotas, parties make a statement. They directly demonstrate to youth that politics is not only the business of old people but that young adults are welcome as well. Third, there could be a contagion effect; if one party nominates (through quotas) a relatively high percentage of youth, other parties could follow suit. With or without quotas, they too might be compelled to support the nomination of youth.

Despite these compelling theoretical accounts, we are skeptical that party quotas are an influential factor for explaining variation in youth representation. Several tendencies support this conjecture. First, voluntary youth quota provisions, regardless of type, are still the exception rather than the rule (see table 4 for a list of countries where at least one party has quota provisions). In fact, we only have identifiable information for seven parties (with a representation of more than seven members) that have a youth quota.[3] These parties are the Social Democratic Party of Croatia, the Democratic Party in Cyprus, the Hungarian Socialist Party, the Social Democratic Party of Lithuania, the Social Democratic Party in Romania, the Social Democrats in Sweden, and the Republican People's Party in Turkey.[4] Second, we could not verify independently how stringent any of the parties are in their application of the voluntary quota provision. After all, to our knowledge, there are rarely penalties if a party does not meet its self-imposed quota provision. Third, parties might adopt quotas for the wrong reasons; they might not be genuinely interested in promoting young adults in office (see Dobbs

---

3. In addition, the German Green Party has what we label a "newcomer quota." This rule dictates that one out of every three consecutive places on the party's list must be filled by a candidate who has not served in a state, federal, or European Parliament. While it is the primary goal of this quota to increase young peoples' representation, we do not count the German Green Party as a quota party, because the quota is not explicitly a quota for the young (see also Reiser 2014). A related rule is present in Sweden's Green Party leadership; their party leaders and party secretary can only hold their posts for ten consecutive years (see https://www.mp.se/om/stadgar).

4. We could not include two parties from two countries listed in table 4. First, the Socialist Peoples' Party of Montenegro only won four seats and was therefore too small to be included in our list of parties. Second, the Partido Revolucionario Institucional (PRI) in Mexico has a 30 percent youth quota for the age group 35 years or under. However, this quota only applies to the upper chamber, the Senate. However, we included the Social Democrats in Sweden, which has set a target that youth should make up one-fourth of all candidates; yet, rather than a formal policy, members have set this target. In reality, the party respects this target, and that is why we include the Social Democrats in the group of parties with party quotas.

2020; Belschner 2021) but rather might adopt them strategically to quell any dissatisfaction or protest by youth or to co-opt young adults (i.e., through the strategy of repression and co-optation). Based on these considerations, we hypothesize that voluntary party quotas should only have a limited influence, if any, on the age composition of party delegations.

The Age of the Party

The age of the party organization is a second party-level factor that might influence the representation of young legislators. Most importantly, we expect that old organizations have long-established networks of commands, consisting mainly of middle-aged and senior men, so-called old boys networks (Dahlerup and Leyenaar 2013; Franceschet and Piscopo 2014). Out-groups, including female and young party members, might have difficulty penetrating these networks, which have formed over decades and which are crucial for the advancement of a political career (Bjarnegård 2013; Bjarnegård and Kenny 2015). In contrast, younger parties are less likely to have developed the same established and close-knit networks, which tend to benefit middle-aged and older men. In these parties, politicians of different ages, including the young, should find a more level playing field. This scenario might be even more probable considering young politicians, who feel alienated by established parties and want to do something new, could be an instrumental force in forming new parties.

Our descriptive evidence at the beginning of the chapter supports the idea that new parties are prone to promote younger representatives; recently created parties are among the frontrunners in youth representation in our sample of 270 party delegations. Our analysis of parties over time in the four countries (Australia, France, Germany, and the United Kingdom) further highlights that new parties have younger parliamentarians, even if this effect fades over time. Hence we expect that the age of political parties matters in explaining variation in the age composition of party delegations.

The Size of Party Support

The third characteristic is the size of the party's support base, which directly influences the party magnitude (i.e., the number of seats the party occupies in parliament). In theory, the party magnitude could be an important characteristic for out-group representation including that of youth. Parties with a small legislative presence, which can count on nominating only a few members to the new parliament after an election, are likely to nominate the type of individual who has the largest appeal to voters. In most cases, actors in gatekeeping positions of parties still think that this "winning candidate" is a middle-aged to senior man (Henig and Henig 2001; Beauregard 2014). Young individuals might therefore not gain much traction if the party magnitude is small. In contrast, parties with larger support might have an incentive to diversify their slates to appeal to as many constituents as possible. This diversification of their list might also entail that they nominate more youth.

Yet the empirical support for the idea that larger parties elect more young adults is far from clear. Our discussion of age representation in party delegations in Australia, France, Germany, and the United Kingdom has shown that the dominant center-left and center-right parties are no front runners in youth representation. In the four countries, these large party delegations have also not increased the legislative presence of youth over the past decades. Rather it seems that new parties, regardless of their parliamentary strength, boost young adults' representation in their party groups. This finding seems to apply regardless of whether these young parties can gain several hundred seats, as was the case for the LREM in the French 2017 elections, or just a couple of seats, as was the case for other parties, such as the Save Romania Union (the party won 13 seats in the parliamentary elections in 2016).

Age of the Party Leader

Party elites are important in the candidate nomination process and the most important person within these organizations is the party leader. In particular, the leader can propel individuals within the party hierarchy and on electoral lists. We see several reasons why young party leaders should promote other young candidates. First, the psychological literature highlights that individuals tend to prefer other individuals that resemble them (Hamlin et al. 2013). According to Crowder-Meyer (2013), this should be especially true for out-group leaders, who might be particularly willing to support members of their own group to control imbalances in representation. As such, young leaders—themselves representing this out-group—might be especially willing to nominate other young adults. Second, the professional and private networks of young leaders should naturally consist of other younger individuals. This reasoning ties into the idea of homophily, the principle that a contact between similar people occurs at a higher rate than among dissimilar people (McPherson et al. 2001). A leader with a larger portion of young individuals in the pool of people deemed as trustworthy and competent should foster their likelihood to nominate younger candidates. Third, and because they are part of an underrepresented generation, young leaders might feel a stronger drive to balance the inequalities in age representation than older leaders. In addition to this direct link, there might also be an indirect connection. Parties that have elected a younger leader might have done so for intergenerational justice reasons, to appeal to younger voters, or to renew themselves. Whatever the reason, if they have elected a young party leader they might also be willing to nominate young candidates.

A quick look at the data seems to confirm the hypothesis that a young party leader might be beneficial for a young party caucus. For example, in our sample the mean and median age of the 36 party delegations that have a party leader aged 40 or lower is under 45 years. In addition, these parties have a disproportionally high share of young parliamentarians. For example, 19 percent of MPs in their party delegations are aged 35 or under and 37 percent of MPs in these groups in parliament are aged 40 years or under. Conversely, the 14 parties with a party leader over 70 years of age tend to have comparatively old parliamentary delegations (i.e., the median age is nearly 54) and fewer legislators aged 35 years or under, as well as aged 40 years or under (the shares are 9 and 14 percent, respectively).

Party Ideology

Finally, we think there are good reasons to theorize about the influence of a party ideology. A party's political ideology is a defining factor of its organization; it matters in regards to which voters a party attracts, the policy programs it adopts, and, if in power, the legislation it passes. In theory, it could also influence the type of representatives a party sends to parliament (Paxton and Kunovich 2003). In more detail, left-leaning parties, which generally support ideas of equality in outcome, could send more young individuals to parliament than parties that are more conservative. In addition, and taken together, young people in the population tend to be more left-leaning. The congruence between a left-leaning party ideology and a stronger support base among younger voters could provide such parties with incentives to present younger lists. However, in practice the dichotomy between left and right might be a little simplistic to explain the age composition of a parliamentary delegation. For example, our descriptive statistics show no major differences in the percentage of youth between the parliamentary groups of center-left and center-right parties. While there are progressive parties on the left, such as green parties, which send younger delegations to parliament (at least in their formative years), there are also leftist organizations, such as communist parties, with some of the oldest parliamentary groups. We also have new left-wing populist parties such as Podemos in Spain, which have a strong youth support base and which are young, and this includes their parliamentary caucus. Given that the empirical record of left and right parties concerning their youth representation seems more complex than a simple dichotomy between left and right, we assume that the party ideology might not be a major factor explaining variation between parties in young legislators. If at all, it might matter moderately, in favor of younger MPs in leftist parties.

4.4. Research Design

The research design to explain variation in our sample of party delegations resembles that of our national country sample (see chapter 3). Analogous to the previous chapter, we present the results of five regression models. On the left-hand side of the five equations are our four dependent variables, the median and mean age of party delegations, and the percent of young parliamentarians aged 35 and 40 years or under. On the right-hand side are the party variables, voluntary party quotas, age of the party, size of party support, age of the party leader, and party ideology.

We operationalized these concepts as follows: the variable *Party quotas* is a dummy, coded 1 if the party has a youth quota in place and 0 otherwise. We constructed this variable predominantly using information from IPU (2018). We tried to verify the information we found in the IPU publication with our own search of online records. We construct our next variable, *Age of party*, by calculating the number of years since the official launch of the party, with the time of the election as the reference data (the data come from Volkens et al. 2017). We gauge the third variable, *Size of party support*, by estimating the vote share the party received at the respective parliamentary election, based on online searches of electoral results. We created the measure *Age of the party leader* by counting the years a party leader has lived at the time of the election (the source was online searches and entries on personal biographies of leaders). Finally, our indicator that captures *Party ideology* is the expert-rated left-right positions of parties from the Manifesto Data (see Volkens et al. 2017).[5]

_____

5. The "rile index," which the Manifesto project uses to calculate left-right positions, is the-

Because of some unavailability in data for a set of data points for the independent variables, we lose about 10 percent of the party units. Our regression models therefore only include 246 observations in 51 countries. As a modeling technique, we use ordinary least squares (OLS) regression with Huber White standard errors. Looking at figure 11, which displays the age distribution across our sample of party delegations across our four age measures, we infer that since graphs one, three, and four are close to normally distributed the choice of OLS is justified when analyzing these variables. Yet the third graph, featuring the percentage of young MPs aged 35 years or under per party delegation, shows a left skew. To control for this skewedness, we add a Tobit model to complement the OLS model for this dependent variable (see model 7a). We also add country fixed effects to all models to account for cross-national factors.

4.5. Results

We have two main party-level factors that influence the average and median age of parliamentarians as well as the share of young legislators. These two indicators are the age of the party and the age of the party leader. Both variables are statistically significant in all models and follow our expected direction (see models 5 to 8 in table 7). For the first factor, the age of the party, we find that our indicator of the number of years since a party's creation moderately influences the mean and median age among MPs in a party delegation. For example, model 6 predicts that a party that is 100 years old has a parliamentary caucus that is on average 1.7 years older than the corresponding caucus of a party that has just come into existence. In addition, the age of the party has some influence on the share of young deputies aged 35 years or under, as well as aged 40 or under. For example, model 8 suggests that a new party that was just created has approximately ten percentage points more MPs aged 40 years or under than a party that is 100 years old; this is a perceptible influence.

The influence of the second statistically significant variable, the age of the party leader, is moderate as well. For instance, according to model 6,

---

oretically bounded by -100 (if a party only mentions left-wing issues in its program) and +100 (if a party only talks about right-wing issues). However, these theoretical minimum and maximum are empirically rare as most parties talk about both left and right issues (however to different degrees), and most parties also mention "neutral" issues that are neither considered left nor right in the rile index (see Volkens et al. 2017).

Table 7. Multiple regression models measuring the effect of party factors on youth representation in political parties

	Model 5 (Mean Age)	Model 6 (Median Age)	Model 7 (35 or under)	Model 7a (35 or under)	Model 8 (40 or under)
Party quotas	.089	.358	−.367	−1.82	3.39
	(1.18)	(1.09)	(3.58)	(5.09)	(5.16)
Age of the party	.016**	.017**	−.068***	−.076***	−.096***
	(.006)	(.007)	(.020)	(.025)	(.027)
Size of party support	−.007	−.007	.032	.118	.060
	(.023)	(0.26)	(.062)	(.075)	(.092)
Age of party leader	.101***	.139***	−.114*	−.148*	−.289***
	(.026)	(.032)	(.068)	(.084)	(.096)
Party ideology	.018	.017	−.076	−.070*	−.113**
	(.015)	(.015)	(.047)	(.042)	(.059)
Rsquared	.48	.50	.30		.38
Log Likelihood				808.57	
Root MSE	3.52	4.23	10.68		14.9
N	246	246	246	246	246

Standard errors in parentheses, *p < .10, **p < .05, ***p < .01 (two tailed). All models include country fixed effects.

the average age of a party's delegation increases by one year for every ten years the party leader's age increases. This means that a party with a leader who is 35 years old should have a delegation that is, on average, three years younger than a party with a leader whose age is 65. Similar to the variable party age, the age of the party leader has a stronger impact on the share of young legislators than on the mean and median age measures. Model 8 roughly predicts that for every year we increase the age of the party leader, the share of young parliamentarians aged 40 years or under decreases by approximately .3 points. In other words, a party with a leader of the age of 40 years should have six percentage points more young legislators in its delegation than a party whose leader's age is 60 years.

The third variable, which has some influence on the age structure in parliaments, is the variable measuring party ideology. Yet the indicator only influences the share of young MPs and not the mean and median age in party delegations, with left-leaning parties having more young legislators. For example, model 8 predicts that for every ten points a party moves toward the right endpoint on the Manifesto project scale we expect its share of young legislators to increase by approximately one point. To take a more concrete example, we could look at the 2017 German federal parliament. The Green Party, which is a left–leaning party, has a score of roughly -21, and the Alternative for Germany, which is a far-right party, has a score of roughly 17. Hence the model would predict that the seat shares of parliamentarians aged 40 years or under in the Green Party is 4 points higher than in the Alternative for Germany (if we were to hold everything else constant), which is a rather small predicted influence.

The descriptive analysis earlier in this chapter has highlighted that communist parties figure on the list of the oldest parties in our sample. The longitudinal analysis of the age structure in France's National Assembly further portrays the French Communist Party as a party with old members. Does this trend apply to all communist parties we study? The answer is yes. The mean and median age of representatives of the seven communist parties in our sample is 55 years. We also replicated models 5 to 8 and exchanged our ideology proxy by a dummy variable for communist parties.[6] This dummy increases the mean and median age (i.e., the dummy coefficient predicts an increase of both the mean and median age of approximately two years). The communist dummy has no influence either statistically or substantively on the percentage of young legislators aged 35 years or under as well as 40 years or under. If we exclude the communist countries from our sample, party ideology becomes statistically insignificant (i.e., $p<.05$) and the substantive influence remains quite weak.

The two remaining variables, party quotas and the size of parliamentary delegation of the party, have no discernable influence on the age structure of party delegations. For both variables, this finding is rather unsurprising. For the first factor, parties tend to apply quotas too selectively, and if they have quota provisions we could not verify independently how strongly these provisions are enforced. In fact, from our sample of roughly 250 parties, only a handful of parties have youth quota rules. However, this also speaks to the potential voluntary party quotas might have in pushing youth representation. If more parties apply these quotas (more stringently), there is a high possibility that youth representation improves in the party delegation and by definition in parliament overall. For the second indicator, the size of the parliamentary delegation of a party, we find no difference in whether they have few or many MPs. This implies that there is no support for the expectation (at least when it comes to young politicians) that larger parties diversify their electoral slates more than smaller parties do. This finding also

---

6. The seven communist parties in our sample are: Czech Communist Party, the French Communist Party, The Leftist Party (Germany), the Greek Communist Party, the Communist Party of India (Marxist), the Japanese Communist Party, and the Russian Communist Party.

contextualizes the PR effect at the national level. Rather than constrained to larger party delegations, the PR effect seems to apply to all parties equally, regardless of whether their parliamentary presence is smaller or larger.

4.6. Discussion

The analysis of political parties adds a more complete picture to our understanding of variation in age representation. In addition to the two national-level institutional factors—the candidate age requirements and, to a lesser degree, PR electoral systems—we discover in this chapter that several party factors matter. The two party factors that have a consistent influence on the age representation of party delegations are the age of the party leader and the age of the party. Most importantly, the age of the party leader has a rather strong influence on the age structure of the party's parliamentary group, with younger leaders being associated with a younger delegation. If we look at our data for roughly 250 parties, we confirm the predictions from the psychological literature and assumptions in research on homophily; that is, younger party leaders tend to elevate other people of roughly their age. They seem to push younger party members to gain candidacy status and election, more so than older leaders. In contrast, it appears that old(er) leaders are likely to push for older candidates. From more of a party perspective, it also makes sense that the same party that is willing to elect a young leader is also willing to send young legislators to parliament. This further implies that if parties care about diversity in age and about intergenerational justice, the nomination of young(er) party leaders could help them become more representative of the general population when it comes to age.

Younger politicians could be agents of change in a second sense. If we think about green parties, or other new parties such as En Marche, younger politicians founded these parties. It is only logical then that these parties also send younger party members to parliament. Yet as these "new" parties mature and establish themselves, they also seem to become parties like others, this includes their age structure. This finding provides another layer to Michels's iron law of oligarchy. Not only do parties over time become more hierarchical but their representatives also seem to get older. It would be interesting to see if these tendencies also apply to the new grassroots parties, such as the Spanish Podemos or the Italian Five Star Movement (M5S), which have formed over the past decade. For example, the membership of Podemos largely consists of a young selectorate of people. Members can enroll online at a very low cost, thus blurring the line between members and sympathizers. Moreover, this party has adopted a design with decentralized candidate selection procedures and digital involvement, favoring the engagement of young people (Peréz-Nievas et al. 2018). Another example is M5S, which has emerged in the wake of the economic crises a decade ago using an antiestablishment narrative. Using online polls and other digital means of innovation, M5S is another "new" political party, whose support is strong among young voters. The party's initial challenge of traditional party cultures has also resulted in a very young pool of candidates (and, indeed, the first time they entered the parliament the party had the youngest group of MPs by far in the Italian Parliament) (Kakepaki et al. 2018).

Will parties like Podemos and M5S permanently renew themselves? Even if young politicians were among the founders of these organizations and even if these parties have structures geared toward young people, it is too early to say if they will maintain their young outlook. One important factor will be if the current elites allow for the periodic renewal in leadership of these parties. In other words, if current party leaders are willing to step aside in five or ten years for the next cohort of leaders, then these new leftist populist parties might continue to nominate young candidates. However, if the current "party elite" decides to stay in power for years and decades to come, then it is likely that the parliamentary delegations of these new parties will soon look like those of other parties. The future will show which of the two conjectures applies to Podemos and M5S. Yet even if they can maintain their young parliamentary caucus, it is far from certain that these leftist populist forces will consolidate their electoral appeal and continue to attract 10, 20, or 30 percent of the vote. In fact, it might be possible that these parties vanish from the political landscape as quickly as they emerged. Again, the future will show which of the two trajectories that will take shape.

Our study also illustrates the unused potential that youth quotas have for increasing youth representation. So far, too few parties selectively apply these measures of positive discrimination to have any impact on the overall age structure in parties or the percentage of young legislators in parliamentary caucuses. However, if applied more frequently and more rigorously, quotas could be a fast-track mechanism to render parliaments more representative of the population in terms of age structure. Unfortunately, we do not think that the political will is there among parties to adopt these corrective measures.

CHAPTER 5

YOUNG POLITICIANS IN CABINET

We have a political problem no one wants to talk about: very old politicians
(HEADLINE OF VOX, AUGUST 7, 2017)

5.1. The Magnitude of Youths' Underrepresentation in Cabinet

Very few people want to talk about youths' underrepresentation in parliaments. This body of research is still small—consisting of about 20 empirical works—especially compared to the hundreds of studies that focus on the presence of women in elected bodies. While at least youths' underrepresentation in parliament is on the agenda of some academics and international organizations, youths' presence in cabinets remains a blind spot. There is literally no one—to our knowledge—who has studied youths' lack of representation in the executive branch: neither international organizations, such as the International Parliamentary Union, nor the academic literature have produced any systematic study of youths' absence in cabinets across the globe. This is surprising, given that a position in the cabinet is the highest office a politician can access. In general, ministers have considerable power, as they are responsible for proposing, formulating, and overseeing most of the laws in their domain (Norris and Lovenduski 1993; Krook 2009). Ministers also sit around the cabinet table and have direct access to the prime minister, chancellor, or president, which in turn might allow them to have some influence on more general policy formulation. This also implies that if young adults want to have influence on policy formation and the adoption of laws, the best place to be would be in the cabinet. Unfortunately, young politicians aged 35 or 40 years or under are largely absent from ministerial portfolios; the presence of youth in cabinet is even lower than their presence in parliament.

In this chapter, we provide an overview of youths' scant presence in cabinets, mimicking the structure of the two previous chapters. We first discuss youth representation in cabinet across a large sample of countries around the world. Second, we hone in on our four cases—Australia, France, Germany, and the United Kingdom—which we study over time. In addition, we present an analysis of the distribution of portfolios that young ministers occupy. Using data that we collected ourselves, we display youths' underrepresentation in ministerial portfolios across a sample of 136 countries around the globe.[1] For each country, we retrieved data for the most recent cabinet at the time we undertook this research. As such, we collected data for cabinets that formed between the years 2013 and 2019. The age data refers to the day of the inauguration of the cabinet.

The first finding that appears is that regardless of how we define young adults, our sample of 136 countries displays that, on average, the compositions of cabinets are even older than parliaments. To illustrate, the median and mean age of cabinet members at the inauguration of each cabinet is approximately four years older than those of parliamentarians (i.e., in our sample the median age of cabinet ministers is 54.79 years and the mean age is 54.67 years). Even more pronounced, young adults are virtually absent from cabinets. The share of cabinet members aged 35 years or under stands at a mere 3.12 percent. Even if we look at ministers aged 40 years or under, our data reveals that less than 9 percent of ministers around the globe are in this age bracket (the exact number is 8.64 percent). This implies that young adults do not even reach half the percentage they reach in parliament, rendering youths' underrepresentation in cabinet endemic.

If we further compare these figures with youths' presence in populations across the globe, the whole dimension of youths' underrepresentation in the highest political office becomes even more palpable. In chapter 3, we calculated that the age bracket 18 to 35 years makes up roughly 28 percent of the voting-age population worldwide. Yet the same age bracket's presence in cabinets across the globe is only slightly more than 3 percent. This gives us a ratio of roughly one to nine if we compare these two figures. If we look at the representation of young adults aged 40 years or under, the ratio slightly improves. Worldometers (2019) estimates that in 2018 the age bracket 18 to 40 years made up roughly 35.5 percent of the voting-age population of the world. If we contrast this number to the 8.64 percent they amass in cabinets, we roughly get a ratio of one to four between youths' representation in cabinet and the share they make of the adult population.[2]

_____

1. Because cabinet members are high-profile individuals, information about their age is often available in the public sphere. To collect these data, we primarily relied on national government websites and complemented this information using websites that record data on recent cabinets, such as news articles and Wikipedia.

2. We must note that these calculations are conservative. If we were to include in our cal-

Similar to youths' presence in parliaments, their underrepresentation in cabinets does not spread equally across all countries. As figure 18 highlights, all four measures of age representation—the mean and median age, as well as the share of cabinet members aged 35 and 40 years or under—display differences between countries. In detail, ranging from a median and mean age of about 40 years to a mean and median age that exceeds 70, there is a variation in the age of ministers. Graphs 1 and 2 in figure 18 further illustrate that most cabinets have a mean and median age between 50 and 60 years old at the time of their formation, but there are also some cabinets at the two tails of the histogram (i.e., at 45 years of age or under and at 65 years of age or higher). If we look at graphs 3 and 4, which focus on the share of youth in cabinets, there is less variation. The mode for both graphs is zero. In other words, 99 cabinets—or 72.79 percent of the sample we cover—have nobody in their ranks aged 35 years or under. For the second age measure, ministers aged 40 years or under, we still have 62 cabinets (45.59 percent of the sample) with no one in this age bracket. However, looking at table 8, we can also identify some bright spots. For example, the Zelensky cabinet, constituted in Ukraine in 2019, has nearly 40 percent of its members aged 35 years or under, and more than 60 percent aged 40 years or under. Another country where young ministers are highly represented is the cabinet in Eswatini (formerly known as Swaziland), which formed in 2018, where one-third of the ministers is 35 years of age or under, and two-thirds of the cabinet are 40 years of age or under.

However, the examples of Ukraine, Eswatini, and those listed in table 8 are the exception rather than the rule. To illustrate, only 30 cabinets have a mean age of 50 or under at the time of their constitution. This number nearly equals the number of cabinets with a mean age over 60 (i.e., 26 cabinets have a mean age above 60) at the time of cabinet formation. If we look at the median age, we have a mere 36 countries in which half or more than half of the ministers are 50 years or under. In the category where half or more than half of the ministers are 60 years of age or older, we have 31 countries. Among "old" cabinets, we also have some cabinets where literally all ministers are "grey," if we look at their hair color. For instance, in four countries—the Philippines (2016), Myanmar (2016), Eritrea (2018), and Nicaragua (2013)—the cabinets have a median age of 70 or higher (see figures 19, 20, and 21 for a graphical visualization of the distribution of youth in cabinets).

---

culations those who do not have the right to vote yet—that is, children and adolescents, who would also more likely benefit from more young representatives—then the ratio between youth representation in cabinets and their share of the larger population in society becomes infinitesimal.

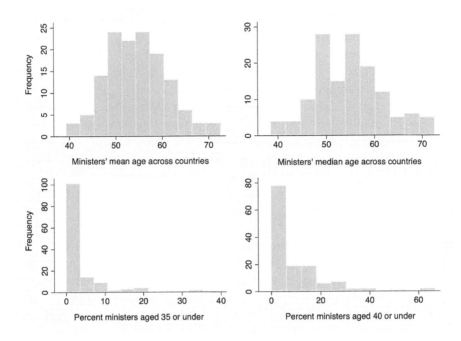

Figure 18. The age distribution in cabinets across the globe in or around 2019

Table 8. Countries with the youngest cabinets

Mean age (years)	Ukraine (39.28), Denmark (41.8), Eswatini (42.17), North Macedonia (42.64), Haiti (44.0)
Median age (years)	Ukraine (38.5), Denmark (40.0), Eswatini (40.0), Haiti (41), North Macedonia (42.5)
Share of ministers aged 35 or under (percent)	Ukraine (38.89), Zimbabwe (33.33), Eswatini (33.33), Finland (21.05), Haiti (20)
Share of ministers aged 40 or under (percent)	Eswatini (66.67), Ukraine (61.36), Denmark (50.0), Albania (40.0), Haiti (40.0)

5.2. Youth Representation in Cabinet over Time in Australia, Germany, France, and the United Kingdom

To study trends over time, we look at our four measures of youth representation in the four selected countries—Australia, France, Germany, and the United Kingdom—over as many cabinets as possible. In fact, we include all cabinets in the four countries in our calculations for which we could get

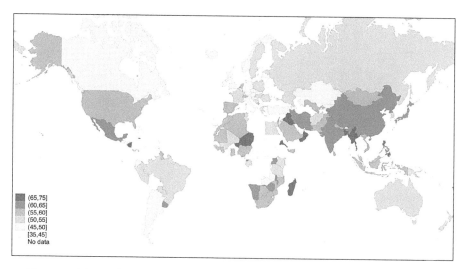

Figure 19. The median age of cabinet ministers across the globe in or around 2019

Figure 20. The percent of cabinet ministers aged 35 years or under across the globe in or around 2019

Figure 21. The percent of cabinet ministers aged 40 years or under across the globe in or around 2019

data, using the same data collection approach and the same type of sources as for our cross-sectional data collection. By graphically visualizing youths' presence across the four countries, we confirm the findings from the four parliaments. That is, similar to the parliaments in Australia, France, Germany, and the United Kingdom, which have not rejuvenated over time, recent cabinets have the same age composition as cabinets 20, 30, or 40 years ago. In fact, for none of the four countries is there any clear upward or downward trend over the past 40 years.

With the exception of Australia, where the mean and median age is slightly lower than 50 years, the mean and median age of the cabinets in the three other countries was higher than 50 years at the time of the inauguration of the cabinet. In more detail, the mean age for all cabinets in Australia (from 1983 to 2019) was 49.1 years, while it was 53.0 years in France (between 1966 and 2018), 52.3 years in Germany (for the years 1983 to 2018), and 52 years in the United Kingdom (for the years 1983 to 2018). The median age in the four countries for the same period is only different in decimals from the mean age. These numbers also confirm the general finding that the age composition of cabinets generally consists of older individuals than parliaments (see figures 22, 23, 24, and 25).

Not only is the majority of cabinet members at the end of their career,

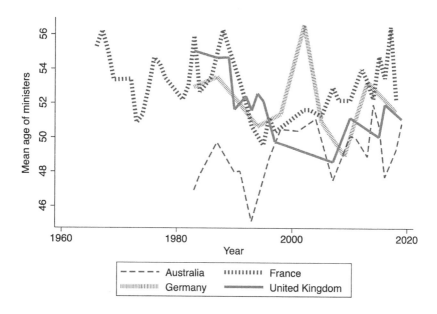

Figure 22. The mean age of cabinet ministers in Australia, France, Germany, and the United Kingdom across time

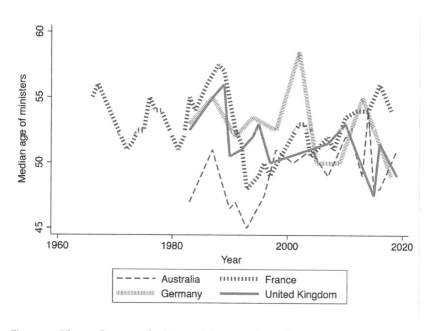

Figure 23. The median age of cabinet ministers in Australia, France, Germany, and the United Kingdom across time

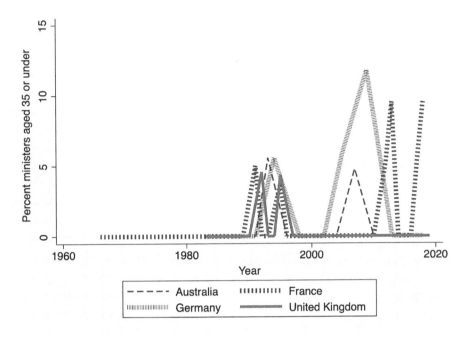

Figure 24. The percent of cabinet ministers aged 35 or under in Australia, France, Germany, and the United Kingdom across time

but young politicians are literally absent from cabinets in these four Western countries. More than 80 percent of cabinets in the four countries have had no minister aged 35 years or under over the past decades (see fig. 24). Given that most cabinets have had an approximate size of 20 members (and sometimes even more), this negligence to nominate young politicians is stunning in a negative sense. In the four countries, young adults aged 18 to 35 make up more than 25 percent of the voting-age population, but in four-fifths of the cabinets this age group has not even had one young minister. This sends a disheartening picture to young adults; they will simply not find anyone they can relate to in their country's cabinet, in terms of age similarity. In fact, the most cabinet posts that young adults, aged 35 years or under, have gained are two ministers in three cabinets (in the 2009 German cabinet, as well as in the 2013 and 2018 French cabinets). Another eight times (out of the more than 80 cabinets), one minister was 35 years or younger at the time of their nomination in the four countries.

Even if we look at the percentage of young ministers aged 40 years or

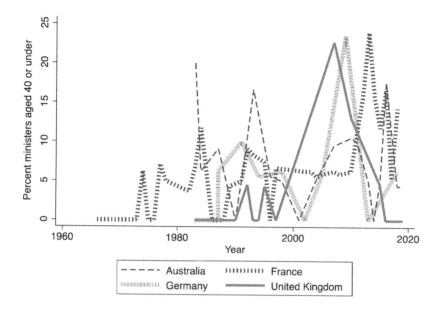

Figure 25. The percent of cabinet ministers aged 40 or under in Australia, France, Germany, and the United Kingdom across time

under at the time of cabinet formation, youths' presence in cabinets is very small (see fig. 25). On average, the 82 cabinets we cover have one person aged 40 or under at the time of her nomination. Since the 1980s, we also do not see any upward trend. In other words, young ministers' absence from cabinet has been a stable feature. Across the time span we cover in these four countries, each country has had only one cabinet with 20 percent or more ministers aged 40 years or under (the 2007 U.K. cabinet, the 2009 German cabinet, the 1983 Australian cabinet, and the 2013 French cabinet). On average, most cabinets we cover had one or two members aged 40 years or under, but in approximately one-fourth of the cabinets, all ministers were older than 40 years. Even in the 2010s, there are still cabinets with zero ministers aged 40 years or under (an example would be the 2016 U.K. cabinet).

Altogether, figures 22 to 25 illustrate the magnitude of youths' underrepresentation in cabinet. Nearly 20 years into the 21st century, young adults aged 35 years or under have a representation rate in cabinet that is close to one to ten relative to their presence in society. For ministers aged 40 years or under, the ratio between youth representation in parliament and youth representation in society is roughly one to five. The examples of Australia, Germany, France, and the United Kingdom illustrate that there has also been no progress in the presence of youth in cabinets. Given the consistency in youths' underrepresentation across various countries, including affluent and less affluent countries, Western and non-Western countries, as well as small and large countries, we believe that other countries have not undergone any progression in youth representation of time in cabinet. In fact, the current low numbers make an increase in the presence of youth impossible. Rather, youths' presence in cabinet has been at the same low rate for four decades in Australia, France, Germany, the United Kingdom, and elsewhere. This also implies that without drastic measures, such as the adoption of mandatory youth representation quotas, youths' lack of representation in parliament, and even more so in cabinet, will persist.

Yet despite youths' flagrant underrepresentation in ministerial portfolios, there is some important variation in the age structure of cabinets. The same applies to how many young ministers sit at the cabinet table. In the next section, we try to explain this variation.

5.3. Explanatory Factors for the Variation in Youth Representation in Cabinet across Countries

What factors explain variation in the mean and median age of cabinets, as well as the share of young ministers? Because there are no prior works that focus specifically on youth representation in cabinets, there is no specific literature on which we can base our expectations. Therefore we build on the literature on other out-groups, our own reasoning, and our findings from youth in parliaments and in party delegations (see chapters 3 and 4). The recruitment to cabinet is different from that of parliament in that the head of the government nominates their cabinet. Hence we have to think about factors that should influence a prime minister, chancellor, or president to assign young adults to cabinet portfolios. We can think of four factors: 1) age representation in parliament, 2) the age of the head of the government, 3) the type of government (i.e., coalition versus majority government), and 4) the size of the cabinet.

Age Representation in Parliament

Research on other out-groups, such as women, has shown that there is a contagion effect between women's representation in parliament and their presence in cabinet. In other words, if women are highly represented in parliament they are also likely to be highly represented in cabinet (Jalazai 2013; Bego 2013). We assume that the same contagion effect might occur between some high youth representation in parliament and some high youth representation in cabinet. Two factors should account for this link. First, high youth representation in parliament signals that parties are willing to support and nominate youth. If they do so in parliament, there is every reason to believe that they will do the same for cabinets. On a related note, high youth representation in the national parliament signals that the country has a political culture that integrates young politicians into decision-making processes. This integration should also happen in the cabinet. Second, there is a more mechanical link between age representation in parliament and age representation in cabinet. Especially in parliamentary systems, the head of the government is often (but not always) bound to nominate ministers from parliament. This implies that with a higher share of young MPs in parliament, we should expect a larger pool of young politicians eligible for ministerial appointments. In presidential systems, this link is rather indirect. In most countries, nominators can select ministers from parliament but have no obligation to do so. For these reasons, we hypothesize that a larger share of youth in parliament should be associated with a higher share of young ministers.

Age of the Head of the Government

In chapter four, we illustrated that the age of the party leader is a significant factor to determine age representation in party delegations. There is an association between younger party leaders and younger parliamentary groups. Here we hypothesize that similar processes should be at stake for cabinet recruitment. The president, chancellor, or prime minister is the most important person when it comes to the selection of ministers. Of course, she must take the voice of party elites into consideration, but beyond that she is relatively free to nominate whomever she deems most competent and adequate for the post. Personal ties often influence considerations for ministerial nominations. There are several reasons why a young head of government would be likely to nominate younger ministers. For one, she might have a natural tendency to nominate ministers closer to her own age. For a cabinet to work well, she must also get along well with her fellow ministers. If the psychological literature is correct, then good working relations are easier with people of the same age group than with individuals from another generation. For these reasons, we believe that young heads of the government have a strong tendency to nominate young(er) ministers. This is reasonable, especially considering that young prime ministers are also more likely to form a coherent group that has shared a similar upbringing and formative culture. In contrast, a very old head of government is likely to have a network of trusted people in line for portfolio assignments.[3] These individuals are likely to be of older age as well. All these reasons make us expect that the age of the head of government influences the age of ministers she selects. On average, younger nominators should select younger minsters.

Coalition Governments

Third, we assume that heads of single-party governments are more likely to nominate youth than heads of coalition governments. Prime ministers and chancellors of coalition governments have a complicated balancing act to perform, since they must assure adequate cabinet representation of all coalition partners (Escobar-Lemmon and Taylor-Robinson 2005). In such a situation, each party sends fewer ministers than it would for a single-party government. This implies that only the most senior party-affiliated names, who are most likely middle-aged to senior men of the dominant ethnicity, are also more likely to receive a cabinet post. In contrast, there are fewer constraints in a single-party government: the head of the government is freer to focus on balancing the cabinet; in theory, she can promote previously underrepresented groups. A more even picture concerning age, ethnicity, and gender might be the result of the cabinet selection procedure.

Size of the Cabinet

Another source of variation might be a country's cabinet size. In our sample of countries, cabinet sizes vary tremendously from smaller than ten people (Luxembourg, Nauru, or Switzerland) to exceeding 50 members (Peru, Russia, or Rwanda). We hypothesize that larger cabinets give the nominator more possibilities to balance the allocation of portfolios according to aspects such as the regional affiliation of ministers, their gender and ethnicity, and their age. For example, if a prime minister has a cabinet of 30 ministers, she might have trouble justifying to the party's youth wing (if one exists) or to young voters more generally the lack of young ministers. In

---

3. For a discussion of the role of trust in cabinet formation, see Stockemer and Sundström (2019e).

addition, in a large cabinet, the head of government can select young ministers without asking senior elites to step aside. In contrast, in a small cabinet,
comprised merely of a handful of members, the seats are more "crowded";
the nominator simply might not have the luxury to diversify her cabinet and
she might want to—or be forced to—select names from the senior party
elite to ministerial portfolios.

5.4. Research Design

To investigate the extent to which these four factors explain variation in the
age distribution of cabinets, we present the results of four multiple regression models, one for each of our dependent variables. We construct our four
independent variables as follows. To operationalize *Youth representation in
parliament,* we use the corresponding indicator for the parliament as we use
for the cabinet (that is, for the first of these models, we use mean age in both
parliaments and cabinets; for the second one, we use the median age, and
so on). As we have illustrated, we collected these figures from parliamentary websites or used the web-scraped data by the EveryPolitician project
(2019). We measure our second variable, *Age of the head of the government*
by the actual age in years of the prime minister, chancellor, or president who
presides over the cabinet, recorded at the time of cabinet formation. *Coalition government* is a dummy variable, coded 1 for a coalition government
and 0 otherwise. The measure for *Size of cabinets* gauges the actual number
of ministers in the cabinet. The data source for the latter three variables is
information from government websites and publicly available data, such as
news sites and Wikipedia.

   We do not include the three institutional measures—youth quotas, electoral system type, and candidate age requirements—because the different
measures of youth representation in parliament should largely capture their
effect. We also do not add the five socioeconomic and cultural variables,
which did not have an influence on youth representation in parliament; that
is, the median age in the population, economic development, corruption,
percent of Muslims in the population, and regime type.[4] We also do not
include a dummy variable for communist governments because none of the
heads of state from our sample comes from a communist party.

---

4. As a robustness check, we include these predictors in our models measuring youths'
   representation in cabinet, but similar to parliaments, none of them has as any significant
   influence on any of our four proxies for age representation in cabinet.

As a modelling technique, we use OLS with Huber White standard errors for the two equations featuring the mean and median age of cabinet members, respectively (see models 9 and 10). Figure 18 illustrates that both median and the mean age of cabinets fit the assumption of a normal curve fairly well. In contrast, the distribution of the other two dependent variables, the percentage of cabinet members aged 35 years or under and those aged 40 years or under, are skewed to the left (i.e., the mode for both variables is 0 and then both variables taper off to the right). This skewed distribution makes Tobit regression models more suitable than OLS regression models (see models 11 and 12). For our univariate statistics (see fig. 18), we have data for 136 countries. Unfortunately, we lose some observations in the multivariate realm because the countries for which we could get parliamentary data often do not match the countries for which we could retrieve data on cabinets (see Appendix 1 and 3). This is why models 9 to 12 only have 91 observations.

5.5. Results

Two factors come out of this analysis as meaningful in explaining variation in the different age measures (see table 9). These two indicators are youth representation in parliament and the age of the head of the government. For the first factor, models 9 and 10 predict that for every year the mean and median age increases in parliament, cabinets become approximately .4 years older, if we hold all other variables constant. Models 11 and 12 further predict that a one point increase in the percentage of parliamentarians aged 35 or 40 years or under is associated with an increase in the percentage of young cabinet members within these two age groups of .57 points and .42 points, respectively.[5]

The second relevant variable, the age of the head of government, also

---

5. In separate specifications, we add a dummy variable for parliamentary system and interact this dummy with the equivalent operationalization of age representation in parliament. This interaction tests whether youth representation in parliament has a stronger influence on youth representation in cabinet in parliamentary systems compared to presidential systems. Theoretically, this link would make sense, considering that in the former type of system the head of the government in many cases must select her ministers from parliament. Yet neither the dummy for parliamentary system nor the interaction term are statistically significant in any of the models. This highlights that there is no difference in the effect of youth representation in parliament on youth representation in cabinet in either parliamentary systems or presidential systems.

Table 9. Multiple regression models measuring the effect of national factors on youth representation in cabinet

	Model 9 (Mean age)	Model 10 (Median age)	Model 11 (35 or under)	Model 12 (40 or under)
Youth representation parliament	.377** (.144)	.427*** (1.62)	.571** (.260)	.421** (.161)
Age of the head of government	.237*** (.044)	.252*** (.053)	−.222 (.153)	−.393** (.156)
Coalition government	.912* (.540)	1.11* (.602)	1.58 (1.88)	.933 (1.83)
Size of cabinet	.007 (.042)	−2.67* (1.47)	.214 (.200)	.216 (.196)
Constant	19.78*** (6.64)	16.32** (7.28)	−4.02 (9.88)	14.07 (10.31)
Rsquared	.42	.40		
Log Likelihood			−152.83	−257.99
Root MSE	4.39	5.05		
N	91	91	91	91

Standard errors in parentheses, *p < .10, **p < .05, ***p < .01 (two tailed). Models 9 and 10 are OLS regression models. Models 11 and 12 are Tobit regression models.

has a substantive influence on the age distribution of cabinets. For instance, models 9 and 10 predict that, on average, a ten-year gap in the age of heads of government between countries, triggers a 2.5 year difference in the mean or median age of cabinets, with those cabinets that have an older chancellor, prime minister, or president also having an older cabinet. Model 12 further predicts that with every year older the prime minister, the share of young legislators decreases by nearly .4 points, which is quite a substantial drop. The third factor, which marginally affects the mean and median age, is the dummy variable for coalition governments. Models 9 and 10 predict that, on average, cabinets in coalition governments have an approximately one year higher mean and median age than cabinets in single-party governments.

In additional specifications, not presented here, we run models 9 to 12 without the variables that measure age representation in parliament, allowing us to include the whole sample of 136 countries. These models confirm the substantive effect of the age of the head of the government and the small effect of coalition governments. This confirmation makes us confident that our more restrictive sample captures the empirical realities that explain the age of cabinet members quite well.

So far the results presented in this chapter offer a rather holistic picture of youths' underrepresentation in cabinets. Yet for an even more nuanced picture of youths' presence in cabinets, it would be interesting to know what ministerial portfolios the few young politicians who make it to cabinet occupy. In the next section, we therefore discuss the type of portfolios that young ministers occupy.

5.6. Cabinet Portfolios of Young Ministers

To determine the type of portfolios that young ministers occupy, we look at the relevancy of portfolios. In other words, we try to measure a minister's relative position in a cabinet. Following the general tendency in the literature to classify portfolios by hierarchies of relevance, such as "core" versus "non-core" or "important" versus "non-important" (see Ono 2012; Claveria 2014; Goddard 2019), we create three categories of cabinet portfolio importance. In more detail, we rely on the well-established work of Escobar-Lemmon and Taylor-Robinson (2005) and distinguish three types of portfolios: 1) high prestige, 2) medium prestige, and 3) low prestige. Analogous to Escobar-Lemmon and Taylor-Robinson, we are rather restrictive in placing a portfolio category in the highest category. In total, we place nine portfolios in the highest category (i.e., Vice Executive, Finance, Foreign Affairs, Government, Public Security, Economy, Interior, Defense, Home Office/Civil Affairs, and Treasury) (see table 10). This portfolio assignment largely mirrors other characterizations that use the terms "hard"/"masculine"/"core" as the highest order of classifications instead of the high-, medium-, and low-prestige typology (Weisberg 1987; Rose 1987; Borelli 2010; Bauer and Tremblay 2011; Krook and O'Brien 2012; Tremblay and Stockemer 2013; Curtin 2014). To be as encompassing as possible, we also present a different—albeit related—classification of portfolio assignment, using the binary distinction between "inner" and "outer" circles (Claveria 2014; Goddard 2019). The "inner" portfolios are the closest advisors to the head of the government and have regular access to the government leader (see table 11).

To get a first idea of age differences in the portfolio assignment we display the mean and median age across high-, medium-, and low-prestige portfolios, as well as inner and outer portfolios. The picture we get is that ministers' age in high-prestige portfolios is an average of approximately three years older compared to cabinet members in medium- or low-prestige portfolios (see table 12). In contrast, there is no age difference between medium- and low-prestige portfolios. The slightly different classification of inner and outer portfolios confirms this finding (see table 13). With a

Table 10. Typology of high prestige, medium prestige, and low prestige portfolios

High prestige	Medium prestige	Low prestige
Finance	Agriculture	Children and Family
Foreign Affairs	Construction and Public Works	Culture
Government	Education	Science and Technology
Public Security	Environment and Natural Resources	Sports
Economy	Health and Social Welfare	Tourism
Interior	Industry and Commerce	Women's Affairs
Defense	Justice	Ministers for reform of the state
Home Office/Civil affairs	Labor	Transient ministries and ministers without portfolio
Treasury	Communications and Information	
Vice Executive	Transportation	

Table 11. Classification of inner versus outer portfolios

Inner portfolios	Outer portfolios
Vice President/Deputy Prime Minister	All other portfolio areas that may not have regular access to the prime minister
Defense	
Finance	
Economy	
Home Office	
Foreign Affairs	

median and mean age of 56 years, on average, inner portfolio ministers are generally three years older than outer portfolio cabinet members.

If we look at young ministers aged 35 years or under, as well as aged 40 years or under, we see that young ministers are less likely to be in the categories of either high-prestige or inner-circle ministers than their older colleagues (see tables 14 and 15). For example, cabinet members aged 35 years or lower have less than a 20 percent chance of presiding over high-prestige or inner-circle portfolio ministries. In contrast, the corresponding likelihood for cabinet members older than 35 years is about 25 percent. While these differences are not tremendous, they nevertheless hint at a double disadvantage: Not only are youth rarely present in cabinet but the few young politicians who succeed in getting a cabinet post also have a lower chance than senior colleagues to be nominated to a prime portfolio.

Table 12. The mean and median age across high-, medium-, and low-prestige portfolios

	High prestige	Medium prestige	Low prestige
Mean age (years)	56.05	53.14	53.37
Median age (years)	56.00	53.00	54.00

Table 13. The mean and median age across inner circle and outer circle portfolios

	Inner circle portfolio	Outer circle portfolio
Mean age (years)	56.04	53.11
Median age (years)	56.00	53.00

Table 14. Youth and the prestige of the portfolio

	High prestige (in % among age group)	Medium prestige (in % among age group)	Low prestige (in % among age group)
Ministers aged 35 or under	17.74	50.00	32.26
Ministers aged 40 or under	21.21	50.00	28.79
Ministers aged 36 or over	25.42	48.30	26.27
Ministers aged 41 or over	25.56	48.22	26.23

Table 15. Youth and the prestige of the portfolio, alternative classification

	Inner circle (in % among age group)	Outer circle (in % among age group)
Ministers aged 35 or under	19.15	80.85
Ministers aged 40 or under	21.00	79.00
Ministers aged 36 or over	27.83	72.17
Ministers aged 41 or over	28.13	71.87

If we look at the portfolio assignment in our four countries over time (Australia, Germany, and the United Kingdom from 1983 to 2018 and France from 1966 to 2018), we have 17 ministers aged 35 or under (of the 1639 ministers for which we could retrieve individual data). Of these 17 ministers, 13 occupy a low-prestige portfolio, one a medium-prestige portfolio (i.e., Health) and three high-prestige portfolios (Defense, Attorney General, and Economy). The most frequent portfolio these young ministers occupy is some variation of the portfolio Family, Women, and Youth (i.e., five times).

To illustrate how infinitesimally small young ministers' presence in high-prestige portfolios is, we calculate the ratio of young ministers in the pool of high-prestige portfolios; one in a hundred ministers in the high-prestige category is 35 years of age or under at the time of her nomination.

In addition, we could identify 128 ministers aged 40 years or under at the time they assumed office. Of these 128 ministers, roughly 40 percent are in the low-prestige category, 34 percent are in the medium-prestige category, and 33 are in the high-prestige category. This finding illustrates that young ministers are somewhat overrepresented in the high-prestige category in the four countries of investigation over time, in comparison to the cross-sectional dataset. This does not mean, of course, that they are overrepresented in comparison to their representation in their age group in the population; it merely means that one of three ministers aged 40 years or under manages to get a top portfolio. When it comes to the specific types of portfolios these young ministers aged 40 years or under occupy, they see their assignment spread throughout all ministries. There is no clear pattern about the type of portfolios young ministers in these countries occupy.

5.7. Discussion

To summarize our findings from this chapter, we can conclude that despite the existence of some young cabinets, such as the Zelinsky 2019 cabinet in Ukraine, young minsters remain an anomaly in most countries in the 21st century. Youths' lack of presence in cabinets is particularly flagrant for politicians aged 35 years or under. This age group occupies less than 4 percent of the cabinet posts in our global sample and just slightly more than 1 percent of the cabinet posts in Australia, France, Germany, and the United Kingdom over the past decades. For ministers aged 40 years or under, the situation is slightly better, but this age group is still represented at a ratio of one to four if we compare their presence in cabinet with their representation in the general population. However, despite these low numbers there is variation in the age of ministers, as well as the percentage of young cabinet members between countries. We mainly explain this variation by two variables—youth representation in parliament and the age of the head of the government. As a rule, cabinets' age decreases with younger parliaments, and younger presidents, prime ministers, and chancellors.

These findings also align nicely with our results featuring youth representation in parliament. For one, it makes theoretical and empirical sense that youth representation in one branch of government (i.e., the legislative branch) affects youth representation in another branch of government (i.e., the executive branch), even more so because in many countries the head of the government selects their ministers from parliament. In addition, we have discovered in chapter 3 that the age of the head of the party affects the age of the party's parliamentary caucus. It is then only consistent that the age of the head of the government affects the age of cabinet members. In the same way, as the party president plays a prominent role in selecting candidates for election, the prime minister, chancellor, and president are primordial in selecting the cabinet. Theoretically, the finding that young nominators have a natural tendency to nominate other young politicians in positions of political power is interesting and complements network composition studies, which illustrate that age is an important factor in shaping peoples' networks (Morgan 1988; Peek and Lin 1999). In politics, it seems that powerful actors tend to surround themselves with their own generation, be it for nomination for legislative office or in selection for executive office.

Hence a possible solution—yet a daunting task—for parties and governments to renew themselves is to select a young politician for their top position. However, young prime ministers and chancellors, such as Volodymyr Zelinsky in Ukraine and Sanna Marin in Finland, are the exception rather than the norm. Most prime ministers and chancellors are in their 50s and 60s, as it generally takes time to reach the pinnacle of power. The distribution of portfolios among different age groups confirms the idea of a long political career as a prerequisite for an influential cabinet post. On average, "high-prestige" or "inner-circle" ministers are three years older than medium- or low-prestige ministers. In addition, there are fewer young ministers in such portfolios, relative to the share of ministers exceeding 35 or 40 years.

CHAPTER 6

YOUTH AS CANDIDATES AND ELECTED REPRESENTATIVES

If young people are not too young to get married, to serve in the military or to choose the parliamentarians who will represent them, they are not too young to run.

(MARTIN CHUNGONG, IPU SECRETARY GENERAL)

6.1. Comparing Candidates and Elected Representatives

So far our empirical chapters have discussed the underrepresentation of youth from the angle of parliaments, party delegations, and cabinets. In this chapter, we take more of an individual perspective and compare the age of (unsuccessful) candidates with the age of elected representatives. We also investigate the factors that predict a candidate's chances of winning a seat. To do so, we use data from the Comparative Candidate Survey (CCS), a joint multinational project that collects data on candidates that run for legislative office in their national legislatures (see CCS 2019). We use the second version of the dataset, which includes information for 21 elections in 17 countries. Because the survey did not include the question of whether somebody was elected in three elections (i.e., Canada in 2015, Australia in 2013, and Estonia in 2015), our sample consists of 18 elections in 14 countries. These elections are Albania (2013), Belgium (2014), Chile (2017), Finland (2015), Germany (2013, 2017), Greece (2015), Hungary (2014), Iceland (2013, 2016, 2017), Montenegro (2012, 2016), Norway (2013), Portugal (2015), Romania (2016), Sweden (2014), and Switzerland (2015). For each country, a national team of researchers sent out the survey to all candidates running in the respective national election. The response rate after several follow-ups was generally between 20 and 50 percent.[1] Since the pollsters took all responses

---

1. We also exclude the 2017 elections in the Czech Republic, for two main reasons: first, the response rate is less than 10 percent, which is significantly lower than that of all other elections, and second, the median age in the study sample is 34, whereas in the median

they could retrieve, the survey cannot claim to be either representative of all candidates or a random selection of candidates or representatives. However, with a total N of more than 11,000 observations, the survey can nevertheless provide a good snapshot of different age groups' representation as candidates and their chances of gaining election.

On the pages to come, we proceed in five steps. First, we compare the mean and median age of candidates who managed to win a seat in parliament with those of unsuccessful candidates. Second, we juxtapose the percentage of unsuccessful candidates aged 35 or under, as well as those aged 40 years or under, with the percentage of successful candidates in the same age cohorts. Third, we build a multivariate model on the predictors of winning a seat. In this model, we are interested in whether age is a relevant factor in explaining somebody's likelihood of being elected. Fourth, we compare the profile of young unsuccessful candidates with that of young representatives. Finally, we contrast young successful candidates with older successful candidates.

6.2. The Average and Median Age of (Unsuccessful) Candidates and Elected Parliamentarians

Tables 16 and 17 highlight that in most elections covered candidates are, on average, younger than elected members of parliament. In more detail, both the median and the mean age of parliamentarians at the beginning of each parliamentary term is approximately three years older for legislators than for unsuccessful candidates (and two years older if we compare legislators to all candidates). In fact, it seems that the only election where candidates are older than elected representatives was in Sweden in 2014. In this election, both the median and mean age are higher in the candidate pool than among those who won a seat. This implies that Sweden in 2014 is the only country in the sample where unsuccessful candidates are, on average, older than successful ones. In addition, Norway (2013) and Belgium (2014) have older groups of candidates compared to representatives, if we look only at the median age. Yet in the two countries the mean age is higher for candidates that make it to parliament than among those that do not win a seat. In all other countries, the candidates who are elected tend to be older than

---

age in parliament is just over 50. This suggests that the respondents are very different from the ones who did not answer the survey.

Table 16. The median age of (unsuccessful) candidates and elected representatives

	Median age of all candidates	Median age of unsuccessful candidates	Median age of elected representatives	Difference (in percentage points)
All countries	47	46	49	3
Switzerland (2015)	41	40	51	11
Hungary (2014)	44	41	48	7
Iceland (2013)	46	45	51	6
Germany (2013)	47	46	50	4
Greece (2015)	50	50	54	4
Iceland (2016)	47	46	50	4
Finland (2015)	52	52	56	4
Iceland (2017)	48	47	50.5	3.5
Montenegro (2012)	48	47	50	3
Montenegro (2016)	43	41.5	45.5	4
Germany (2017)	51	50	52	2
Albania (2013)	46	44	46	2
Romania (2016)	43	43	44	1
Portugal (2015)	45	45	45.5	0.5
Chile (2017)	49	49	49.5	0.5
Belgium (2014)	46.5	47	46	−1
Norway (2013)	46	46	44.5	−1.5
Sweden (2014)	49	50	48	−2

unsuccessful candidates, regardless of whether we look at the median or mean age. Sometimes these differences are substantive, as in the case after the 2015 Swiss elections: the median and mean age are approximately ten years higher for successful candidates as compared to unsuccessful ones. At other times, the discrepancy is minimal. An example would be the 2016 Romanian election, where the difference in age between parliamentarians and unsuccessful candidates is only about one year, regardless of whether we take the mean or median age.

How can we explain this older age of successfully elected legislators compared to unsuccessful candidates? Since our dataset does not offer us the complete candidate registrar, we could not retrieve information on the list position of any candidate, or on the type of district in which the survey participants ran. Therefore we cannot determine whether the parties, the voters, or both are responsible for this disadvantage against young candidates. If it is the parties, it is likely that they put younger candidates in party list positions with low chances of ever reaching office, or in districts that the respective party cannot win. If it is the voters, they might actively choose

Table 17. The mean age of (unsuccessful) candidates and elected representatives

	Mean age of candidates	Mean age of successful candidates	Mean age of elected representatives	Difference (in years, between unsuccessful and successful candidates)
All countries	46.14	45.49	48.33	2.84
Switzerland (2015)	41.16	40.67	49.51	8.84
Iceland (2013)	46.21	45.40	53.34	7.94
Germany (2013)	45.94	44.96	49.77	4.81
Hungary (2014)	44.41	42.62	47.39	4.77
Greece (2015)	49.50	49.12	53.79	4.67
Iceland (2017)	48.94	47.46	51.86	4.4
Montenegro (2012)	46.25	44.91	49	4.09
Montenegro (2016)	43.17	42.31	46.11	3.8
Germany (2017)	48.67	48.06	50.70	2.64
Iceland (2016)	47.13	46.95	49.5	2.55
Albania (2013)	43.89	43.22	45.70	2.48
Norway (2013)	44.92	44.92	47.39	2.47
Belgium (2014)	46.16	45.99	47.69	1.7
Finland (2015)	49.73	49.51	50.74	1.23
Romania (2016)	44.23	44.02	45.13	1.11
Portugal (2015)	46.08	45.74	46.36	0.62
Chile (2017)	48.92	48.81	49.21	0.4
Sweden (2014)	49.73	49.01	45.93	−3.08

senior candidates instead of junior ones, no matter their placements on lists or districts.

6.3. The Share of Young (Unsuccessful) Candidates and Legislators

If we look at the ratio between young contenders that are unsuccessful and young representatives, the disadvantage of being young in elections becomes apparent. For example, throughout our sample of 18 elections, roughly 25 percent of candidates are 35 years or under at the time of the election (see table 18). In other words, slightly more than one out of four candidates are in this age category when running for office. A ratio exceeding one to four between the candidates at or under 35 years of age and those above this benchmark suggests that the supply of young candidates is surprisingly high. This relatively high number also suggests that there is no systematic discrimination of youth at candidacy. Yet the picture is different if we look at elected parliamentarians. The group of young adults as a share

Table 18. The percent of unsuccessful and successful candidates aged 35 years or under

	Share of candidates aged 35 or under (in %) of all candidates	Share of unsuccessful candidates aged 35 or under (in %) of all unsuccessful candidates	Share of elected representative candidates aged 35 or under (in %) of all elected representatives	Difference (in percentage points) between unsuccessful and successful candidates
All countries	25.36	28.14	13.39	−14.75
Switzerland (2015)	42.12	43.96	10.20	−33.76
Iceland (2017)	22.34	26.96	0	−26.96
Montenegro (2012)	19.85	26.44	5.26	−21.18
Iceland (2013)	24.86	27.08	6.90	−20.18
Belgium (2014)	25.90	27.88	7.96	−19.92
Germany (2013)	21.99	25.41	8.62	−16.79
Hungary (2014)	23.79	29.83	13.79	−16.04
Iceland (2016)	23.30	24.31	9.09	−15.22
Germany (2017)	19.43	22.85	8.06	−14.79
Montenegro (2016)	35.12	38.43	23.68	−14.75
Albania (2013)	21.19	24.42	12.50	−11.92
Romania (2016)	24.87	26.50	18.18	−8.32
Portugal (2015)	20.39	24.31	16.68	−7.63
Greece (2015)	13.56	14.15	6.90	−7.25
Finland (2015)	21.81	22.60	17.39	−5.21
Norway (2013)	26.96	27.14	24.07	−3.07
Chile (2017)	16.00	16.11	15.71	−0.4
Sweden (2014)	21.90	21.37	27.20	5.83

of all winning contestants in our sample drops significantly to roughly 13 percent, suggesting that there is, indeed, a systematic disadvantage facing young adults.

Young candidates also have a lower chance of winning a seat than more senior ones. In more detail, our sample includes 2,840 candidates aged 35 years or under. Of these 2,840 people, 199 won their election. This tells us that the chance of winning for any candidate at or under 35 years of age is about 7 percent. If we compare this likelihood of winning a seat to the likelihood among more senior contestants, we see that older candidates have a higher chance of winning. To illustrate, we have 397 successful candidates in our sample aged 55 to 65 and 1,700 unsuccessful ones in this age bracket in our sample. This translates into a 19 percent chance of winning a seat for these more senior candidates.

There is also wide variation in the distribution of unsuccessful and successful candidates aged 35 years or under between countries (table 18). In some countries, such as Switzerland and Iceland, the gap between the percentage of those candidates who win or lose is very large. For instance, in the 2015 Swiss elections, nearly one in two candidates was 35 years or under. This means that young people were overrepresented as candidates in comparison to other age cohorts. Yet among those that were elected to parliament, the same age category only made up about 10 percent. Iceland, particularly in the elections of 2017, is another example of flagrant discrepancy between the percentage of young candidates and the percentage of young representatives. In the 2017 elections, candidates aged 35 years or under made up more than 22 percent of the sample of all candidates who took the survey but won none of the seats.[2] Once again, we can ask the question: who is to blame for this disadvantage—parties or voters? The answer is probably both. In Switzerland, parties present lists in every canton and voters rank candidates on the party list, thus changing the order. Therefore it seems that voters in those settings prefer older candidates. However, this finding comes with the caveat that turnout in elections for the Swiss National Council is generally among the lowest in any industrialized country, around 50 percent (see Blais 2014). Nevertheless, young candidates seem to underperform in comparison to the ones that are more senior.[3]

Yet in other contexts, it is more likely that the parties are to blame for young candidates' underperformance. For example, Iceland has closed list proportional representation (Kedar et al. 2016). As such, parties determine the list position of anyone running and, by voting for a list, voters must accept the rank of candidates on this list. Hence there is some strong evidence that, in Iceland, parties are willing to put young candidates on their lists but often in positions where they stand no real chance of winning the election. Of course, this potentially sends an unpleasant signal to youth: they are welcome as tokens on a list but less welcome as elected members of parliament.

Despite the large discrepancy between the number of young contenders and the number of seats that young candidates win in most contexts, there seems to be a handful of countries that promote young candidates.

2. From the website EveryPolitician, it seems that two MPs elected in 2017 were born in 1982 and 1983, respectively. However, it seems that these two MPs did not take the survey and thus do not feature in the CCS data.

3. A list for the Swiss National Council normally includes as many people as there are seats to distribute in a canton. A voter can either vote for the list, in which case any candidate gets one vote, or alternatively can split votes between lists by voting for candidates. For every list, the candidates with the most votes get elected.

The prime example is Sweden (i.e., the 2014 election). Compared to most other countries, we can observe a rather low share of young adults in the candidate pool. Yet if we look at the group of successful candidates, this age cohort was often successful. In fact, the ratio of young winners as a share of all winners surpasses the ratio of young unsuccessful candidates as a share of all such unsuccessful candidates in our survey. The Swedish system is, for the most part, an open list PR system. There is a proposed ranking on the party list, but voters can change this ranking by actively choosing any name on these lists. The electoral lists also show the age of each candidate. This implies that voters can actively promote younger or older candidates without necessarily knowing them. Thus it seems that the relative advantage that young candidates have is twofold. First, parties promote young candidates on lists by placing them relatively high up on these lists. In addition, voters do not seem to disadvantage younger candidates.

If we look at the second age measure, candidates aged 40 years or under, we confirm the discrepancy between youth among unsuccessful candidates and youth among successful ones (see table 19). Yet the gap between the percentage of losing candidates compared to all candidates and winning candidates compared to all elected representatives within this same age group is not as wide as for those aged 35 years or under. This might imply that parties and voters do not consider candidates in their late thirties as young anymore and give them better chances in nomination contests. Between countries, we see the same wide variation as for the measure aged 35 or under. In some countries, the discrepancy between the share of candidates among unsuccessful ones and the share of winners within all legislators is flagrant in the survey sample. Examples are the aforementioned Switzerland (2015), but also Greece (2015) and Germany (2017). For instance, our survey data indicates that in the 2015 Greek elections the percentage of young candidates was already quite low. Only roughly one out of five candidates was 40 years or younger at the time of the election. Yet this ratio dropped to roughly one to 14 for elected members of parliament. This indicates that in Greece's proportional list system, the parties did not nominate many young candidates, and the majority of those they did nominate were placed in ineligible list positions. In Germany, we have a similar picture for the 2017 elections: relative to older individuals, there were ten percentage points fewer young individuals among the members of parliament pool in our survey than in the candidates' pool. In the mixed member proportional representation system in Germany, it appears that parties are hesitant to nominate young candidates on both direct winnable seats and on eligible list positions.

Table 19. The percent of (unsuccessful) candidates and legislators aged 40 or under

	Share of all candidates aged 40 or under	Share of unsuccessful candidates aged 40 or under (in %) of all candidates	Share of successful candidates aged 40 or under (in %) among all legislators	Difference (in percentage points) between unsuccessful and successful candidates)
All countries	35.25	37.50	26.09	−11.41
Iceland (2013)	36.72	40.28	10.34	−29.95
Switzerland (2015)	49.27	50.83	22.43	−28.4
Iceland (2017)	32.73	36.21	9.09	−27.12
Montenegro (2012)	32.06	39.08	23.68	−15.4
Greece (2015)	20.34	21.53	6.90	−14.63
Germany (2013)	32.28	35.25	20.69	−14.56
Iceland (2016)	35.52	36.84	22.73	−14.11
Hungary (2014)	42.76	47.51	34.86	−12.65
Germany (2017)	27.40	30.31	17.74	−12.57
Belgium (2014)	35.54	36.67	24.64	−12.03
Albania (2013)	31.78	34.88	23.44	−11.44
Montenegro (2016)	46.43	48.46	39.47	−8.99
Romania (2016)	41.12	42.27	36.36	−5.91
Portugal (2015)	33.88	36.81	31.25	−5.56
Norway (2013)	35.33	35.33	35.19	−0.14
Chile (2017)	26.00	25.56	27.14	1.58
Finland (2015)	32.38	32.45	34.78	2.33
Sweden (2014)	31.24	30.60	37.60	7

As for those aged 35 years or under, this pattern of youths' underperformance as candidates does not apply to all countries for the age group 40 or under. The prime example of a country where young candidates outperform senior candidates is, again, Sweden, having 31 percent of adults aged 40 or under on electoral lists in the sample. Yet the 37 percent young legislators aged 40 or under makes Sweden one of the countries with the youngest representatives. The two other countries where the ratio of young to more senior candidates reflected the ratio of young to more senior representatives were Chile and Norway. Therefore parties in Sweden, and to a somewhat lesser degree in Chile and Norway, show young adults and everyone else that they promote youth by giving them more of a fair chance on their lists.

Tables 18 and 19 also debunk a myth about youths' underrepresentation. At least among respondents of the survey, young candidates seem to exist in rather high numbers. In nearly every election in our data, the ratio between young candidates and older candidates reflects, or comes close to, the ratio between young(er) and old(er) citizens in the respective populations. The fact that we have 25 percent of candidates aged 35 or under and 35 percent of candidates aged 40 or under seems to illustrate that young candidates are willing and motivated to run in elections. Hence narratives that describe youth as lacking ambition to engage in formal politics or lacking the willingness to run for elections, which are a relatively frequent feature in studies of the United States (e.g., Lawless and Fox 2015), do not necessarily hold true in a comparative perspective. This insight also adds nuance to our theoretical framework, which we presented in chapter 2. As least in some Western countries, youth are not absent as candidates; instead the problem is that most young candidates do not win a seat.

More normatively and, this time in strong support of our theoretical framework (see chapter 2), tendencies of parties to take young candidates seriously might alleviate the vicious cycle of political alienation, while reversed practices might promote it. In our analysis, both Sweden and Switzerland came off as endpoints on the spectra on which young adults are advantaged or disadvantaged in electoral races. Table 20 compares the political interests of young citizens aged 35 or under in Sweden, where young candidates are at an advantage in elections, with those in Switzerland, the setting in this sample where young candidates seem to face the largest disadvantage. Contrasting political interest levels among young adults in the two countries and using data from the European Social Survey, we find stark differences. In Sweden, nearly 60 percent of young adults aged 35 or under report that they are either "very" or "quite" interested in politics. In Switzerland, about 20 percent of the polled young adults responded in an affirmative way to this question. This contrasting pattern can have multiple reasons related to civic education in school, the institutional contexts, and the general political culture in the two countries. Nevertheless, the fact that political parties in Sweden actively support young candidates and allow them adequate representation might also signal to young people that they too have a say in politics; this, in turn, might encourage them to seek political information and to become politically educated and involved citizens.

6.4. The Age Factor in Explaining the Success of Candidates

6.4.1. Research Design and Methods

So far we have ample descriptive evidence that, with some exceptions, young candidates in our sample have lower chances of winning elections

Table 20. Political interest of the 35 years old or under in Sweden and Switzerland

Interested in politics	Sweden		Switzerland	
	Percent	Cum. Percent	Percent	Cum. Percent
Very interested	11.96	11.96	2.85	2.85
Quite interested	46.47	58.52	18.52	21.37
Hardly interested	35.60	94.02	44.44	65.81
Not at all interested	5.71	99.73	34.19	100
Do not know	.27	100	0	100

Comment: The data come from the 2018 version of the European Social Survey (see ESS 8).

than more senior ones. In this section, we investigate the effect of age on the likelihood of candidates winning a seat in a multivariate framework. To do so, we present several logistic regression analyses, with country fixed-effects. In models 13 to 15, we regress the binary variable "elected" or "not elected"—again using information from the CCS dataset—on three age proxies; the actual age of survey respondents, a dummy variable coded 1 if the respondent is aged 35 or under, and a dummy variable coded 1 if a candidate is 40 years or under. In models 16 to 18, we add five additional predictors, which should also influence a candidate's likelihood of winning a seat. These five variables are electoral capital, party capital, encouragement to run, endorsements, and gender.

First, we suggest that the electability of candidates increases with their electoral resources (Murray 2008); that is, sitting members of parliament or politicians in other high echelon electoral positions should have an electoral advantage. They have high visibility, staff to prepare the electoral campaign, and experience. All of this should increase their chances of winning. Our variable *Electoral capital* is a five-value ordinal variable. We code this variable 0 if the candidate has never held any electoral or governmental office, 1 if the candidate has held electoral office at the local level, 2 if they have been a mayor, 3 if the candidate has served in the regional parliament or government, and 4 if the candidate has served in the national parliament/government or in the European Parliament. In cases where a candidate has held electoral offices at various governmental levels, we count the highest office any candidate has ever held.

Based on a similar reasoning, we think it plausible that the electability of candidates increases with their experience in a party (Hassell 2016). We measure *Party capital* as a five-value ordinal variable, coded 0 if the candidate has never held any party office, 1 if the candidate has worked for a party as an unpaid volunteer, 2 if the candidate has worked as a paid party/campaign worker or employee under an MP, 3 if they have held a local or regional party office, and 4 if the candidate has held any national party office. Again we code an individual with information on the highest office they have held. Third, we also find it probable that candidates who have been encouraged to run by interest groups or influential individuals would tend to outperform candidates who have not (Pruysers and Blais 2018). To measure our fourth variable *Encouragement to run,* we construct a dummy variable, coded 1 if the candidate has received some encouragement to run and 0 otherwise. Another feature that we believe to matter is whether a candidate has received endorsements. We hypothesize that an individual contender that has gained such support should be more likely to win a seat compared to a candidate without endorsements (Cancela et al. 2017). We operationalize *Endorsements* as a dummy variable, coded 1 if the candidate has received any official endorsement from important actors (e.g., trade union, industry, civil society organizations, etc.) and 0 if they have not received this type of support. Finally, we find it likely that gender matters. Formal politics is still largely a male domain that women face difficulties in assessing (i.e., around 75 percent of the members of the lower houses across the globe are men); this male dominance should also give an advantage to male candidates over female ones (Sanbonmatsu 2020). To capture *Gender,* we create a dichotomous variable, coded 1 for men and 0 for women. The data source for all these individual-level variables is the CCS (2019).

When interpreting the models, we should keep in mind that if there is a correlation of any of these controls with age, then models 13 to 15 should "underestimate" the effect of age due to multicollinearity (see also section 6.5). For all models, we also present some probability plots of the variable age in order to interpret the substantive influence of the logistic regression coefficients.

6.4.2. Results

Table 21 and figure 26 confirm the descriptive statistics; that is, the age of a candidate matters for their chances of winning an election. All three proxies of age are in the expected direction. Age increases a candidate's likelihood of winning in a statistically significant manner (see models 14, 15, and 16). More substantively, the three graphs in figure 26 display the predicted effect of age on somebody's likelihood of winning, based on models 14 to 16. For

Table 21. Bivariate logistic regression analyses measuring the influence of age on a candidate's chance of winning a seat in parliament

	Model 14	Model 15	Model 16
Age	.016***		
	(.002)		
35 or under		−.816***	
		(.083)	
40 or under			−.492***
			(.067)
Constant	−2.52***	−1.21***	−1.22***
	(.103)	(.075)	(.076)
Log Likelihood	−3749.72	3720.37	−4191.68
Pseudo Rsquared	.11	.12	.11
N	10542	10542	10542

Standard errors in parentheses, *p < .10, **p < .05, ***p < .01 (two tailed). All models include country fixed effects.

instance, the first graph highlights that the chances for somebody to win a seat are nearly twice as high when the person is in their 60s than when the person is in their 20s. If we look at the second graph, we get confirmation of youths' lower chances of winning an election. Individuals aged 35 years or under at the time of election have about half the likelihood of winning a seat in the national parliament compared to people over 35 years of age. For individuals aged 40 or under at the time of election, the gap is a bit less pronounced. Yet model 16 still predicts a 50 percent higher chance of winning for candidates aged 40 or over compared to those aged 40 or under. Hence these illustrations confirm the disadvantage of being young when running for office. Moreover, we confirm findings from prior chapters that people aged 35 years or under are even less advantaged in comparison to those in the age span 40 years or under. In other words, these figures suggest that after the age of 35, a candidate's chances of winning a seat tend to increase.

We get a somewhat different picture if we look at table 22 and figure 27. When we add the five predictors—electoral capital, party capital, encouragement to run, endorsements to run, and gender—age has a much weaker influence on a candidate's chance of winning than in the bivariate analyses. In more detail, the predicted substantive effect of the dummy variable gauging those aged 35 years or under, while still statically significant (p < .001), is about half the size of that in the bivariate realm (see graph 2 in fig. 27). In addition, the first graph in figure 27 indicates that the effect of age (measured

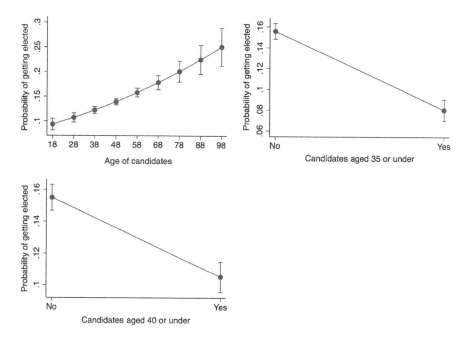

Figure 26. The probability of election for different operationalizations of age (bivariate model)

as a continuous variable) has largely flattened out after adding the controls. The same applies for the dummy variable aged 40 years or under; after the addition of the control variables, this variable is no longer statistically significant either. This declining impact points to a correlation between age and at least one of the three factors that drive somebody's chances of winning a seat (i.e., electoral capital, party capital, and endorsements). In models 17, 18, and 19, the strongest predictor is electoral capital. If we standardize the effects of electoral capital, party capital, and endorsement in these models (see Long and Freese 2005), the standardized logistic regression coefficient for electoral capital is twice as high as the standardized coefficient for the other two significant variables. This finding might have relevance for the broader implications of our study. If younger candidates have less electoral capital than older ones, we might have a prominent explanation for why they have lower chances of winning a seat. We discuss the degree to which this is the case in the next section. In addition to electoral capital, we also discuss whether age influences the party capital of candidates and the extent to which young candidates receive endorsements.

Table 22. Multiple logistic regression models measuring the effect of individual factors on a candidate's chances of winning a seat in parliament[1]

	Model 17	Model 18	Model 19
Age	.0002		
	(.003)		
35 or under		−.377***	
		(.090)	
40 or under			−.111
			(.073)
Electoral Capital	.483***	.459***	.475***
	(.023)	(.022)	(.022)
Party Capital	.228***	.236***	.230***
	(.032)	(.032)	(.032)
Encouragement	−.020	−.020	−.017
	(.077)	(.077)	(.077)
Endorsement	.251***	.251***	.248***
	(.094)	(.094)	(.094)
Gender	−.081	−.081	−.082
	(.081)	(.069)	(.069)
Log Likelihood	−3302.84	−3293.64	−3301.68
Pseudo Rsquared	.20	.20	.20
N	10373	10373	10373

Standard errors in parentheses, *p < .10, **p < .05, ***p < .01 (two tailed). All models include country fixed effects.

1. We did not include education in the model, because there is very little variation in the educational level of candidates. Roughly, four out of five candidates have some university education. In addition, there is no variation in the educational standard between older and younger candidates.

6.5. Characteristics of Young and Older Candidates

Model 18 in table 22 has brought three indicators to the fore that influence candidates' chances of winning a seat: electoral capital, party capital, and whether the candidate secured at least one endorsement. In this section, we discuss how any of these factors correlates with age.

Electoral Capital

For the strongest factor in the regression models, electoral capital, we see a strong linkage with age. Table 23 clearly reveals that young candidates do not have the same amount of electoral capital as their more senior counterparts. To illustrate, more than two-thirds of the candidates aged 35 or under do not have any electoral experience; they have not held office at the local, regional, or national level. For candidates over 40 years of age, the percent-

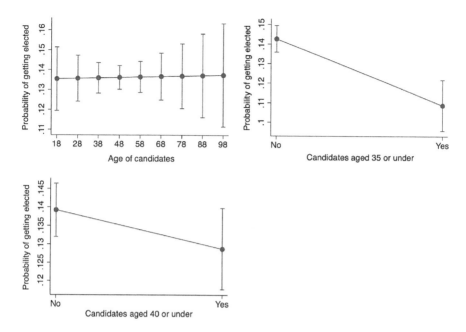

Figure 27. The probability of election for different operationalizations of age (multivariate model)

age drops to around 40 percent. Inspecting those who have held a seat at the national level, European level (where applicable), or previously held an appointed national government position, only roughly one out of ten young candidates aged 35 or under has had this experience prior to being a candidate for the national elections. In contrast, focusing on the candidates older than 40 years, roughly one in four candidates has held some national-level or European-level elected position or has worked in the national government before accepting candidacy for the national parliament.

If we look at the last row, which displays the share of candidates who are sitting incumbents, the gap between age cohorts becomes even more pronounced. Within the age bracket of those aged 35 years or under, less than 4 percent of candidates are sitting incumbents. For candidates aged 40 years or under, the percentage of incumbents is slightly higher; it stands at nearly 6 percent. Yet for the candidates who have passed the bar of 40 years, the rate of incumbency increases steeply: roughly 20 percent have already held a seat in parliament (i.e., 16 percent for those aged 40 to 55 and 23 percent for those over 55). Our study therefore confirms the finding in the

Table 23. The electoral capital of candidates across various age brackets (responses in percent)

	35 or under	40 or under	40 to 55	Over 55
Candidate has never held any electoral office	67.22	61.68	39.36	41.27
Candidate has held electoral office at the local level	18.52	19.79	24.18	21.68
Candidate has been a mayor	.46	1.09	3.93	3.25
Candidate has held an elected job or a government job at the regional level	3.52	4.00	6.83	6.64
Candidate has held an elected job or a government job at the national level	10.28	13.44	25.70	27.16
Sitting incumbent	3.63	5.92	15.87	22.67

literature that incumbents have a tremendous advantage at the ballot box, with reelection rates of more than 80 percent in some countries, including the United States (e.g., Cox and Katz 1996; Praino and Stockemer 2012). In our sample, the reelection rate of incumbents is 69 percent. Hence there is some evidence that incumbency serves as an impediment for the election of young candidates. Yet this finding comes with some important nuance. For other out-groups, such as women, research has identified that the incumbency advantage can dissuade female candidates from running in elections (e.g., Palmer and Dennis 2001). For youth, this is not necessarily the case. In the sample that we study, young adults actually do seem to run for office; however, more often than not, they fail to win a seat. This finding applies at least to Western countries; for non-Western countries, there is so far not enough data to compare youth in the candidate pool and youth in elected office. Therefore, at least for the West, the incumbency advantage and electoral capital are factors that prevent young politicians from winning a seat. More generally, this implies that most of the young candidates do not have the necessary experience to be competitive in the electoral market.

Party Capital

If we look at the party capital of candidates in different age brackets, we find very little difference between age groups (see table 24)—that is, young

Table 24. The party capital of candidates across various age brackets (responses in percent)

	35 or under	40 or under	40 to 55	Over 55
Candidate has neither worked for a party nor held any party office	13.56	14.10	15.28	20.67
Candidate has worked for a party as an unpaid volunteer	19.51	18.86	14.04	11.35
Candidate has worked as a paid party/campaign worker or MP employee	3.59	3.52	1.98	1.29
Candidate has held a local or regional party office	42.11	41.91	46.43	41.69
Candidate has held a national party office	21.23	21.61	22.28	25.00

candidates do not show less activism or experience in parties compared to older candidates. For example, it is quite impressive that more than 60 percent of young candidates aged 35 years or under, as well as those aged 40 or under, have held some party office before running for parliament. This share of candidates aged 40 or under with experience in party leadership is equivalent to the share of candidates aged 40 or over who have held party office. It is even more telling that the age bracket of under 35 has the fewest individuals never having worked for a party, even if these differences between various age groups are small. This indicates that young candidates are equally or even slightly more active in their parties than candidates that are more senior. Yet this high level of engagement within the party structures does not seem to translate into equal representation. It might give them candidacy, but more often than not this candidacy does not translate into winning a seat in parliament. For the broader engagement of youth in parties, table 24 also points to a feature not much discussed in the literature: that is, young adults might be a minority in political parties but those who are party members are willing to take on party leadership positions and run for elected office.

Endorsements

Table 25 illustrates that little difference exists when it comes to the number of endorsements candidates of different age brackets receive. In fact,

Table 25. Endorsements across various age brackets (responses in percent)

	35 or under	40 or under	40 to 55	Over 55
Candidate has received at least one endorsement	7.75	7.82	11.04	6.97

the data reveal that most candidates, whether younger or older, have not received any endorsements. It seems that in list proportional systems, civic organizations do not endorse candidates but parties. Even in majoritarian systems, the endorsements seem to go to the candidate for prime minister or president and not to the individual candidates running for a seat in parliament. Yet, as models 17, 18, and 19 show, if candidates can secure an endorsement they tend to see increased election chances. However, and this is important for our study, candidates aged 40 or under seem to be (nearly) as skilled in securing an endorsement as candidates in their late 40s and early 50s.

6.6. Electoral Capital of Young(er) and Older Successful Candidates

At the age of 25, 30, or 35, young politicians are active within parties, but most of them have not managed to win a seat. So far we know that regardless of the age group, the chances of candidates with electoral capital (in particular, national-level political experience) of getting a parliamentary seat are higher than the chances of those without electoral capital (see table 26). By comparing the distribution of younger successful candidates with older ones, this section offers some complementary evidence of the importance of electoral capital. For example, the gap in the number of successful candidates with no electoral experience or electoral experience at a lower level is moderate across various age brackets. However, if we look at the last row, we see that there are approximately six times as many successful candidates with national-level electoral experience in the 40 to 55 age group and five times as many winning contenders in the over 55 age group as compared to the 35 or under age group. Therefore table 26 provides further evidence for the salience of electoral capital. To a large part, young candidates are disadvantaged in elections to parliament because they do not have national-level electoral experience. It also seems that parties do not factor in the incumbency advantage in their decision to nominate candidates for eligible seats by, for example, having some compensatory mechanism that

Table 26. Successful candidates by electoral capital (responses in absolute numbers)

	35 or under	40 or under	40 to 55	Over 55
Candidate has never held any electoral office	74	121	123	84
Candidate has held electoral office at the local level	58	102	129	31
Candidate has been a mayor	1	7	37	31
Candidate has held an elected job or a government job at the regional level	13	22	42	37
Candidate has held an elected job or a government job at the national level	53	131	326	279

balances youths' discrimination based on the incumbency advantage. One such compensatory mechanism could be that half the spots on party list or district candidacies must go to nonsitting candidates.

6.7. Discussion

Using data from the CCS, we have shown in this chapter that a significant number of young candidates seem to be willing to run for national office and parties are prepared to nominate them on lists or as direct candidates. Young candidates in this sample also show few differences with their more senior colleagues, at least when it comes to party capital and the number of endorsements they receive. They are active in parties and most of them have held party office before running for national legislative office. Nevertheless, young politicians face strong underrepresentation in parliaments across the globe. Our analysis suggests that this underrepresentation stems partly from the fact that young candidates have lower chances of winning a seat than those from older generations. A prominent explanation for this underrepresentation is that the average young candidate has lower electoral capital than the average more senior candidate does. In our regression model, electoral capital is the most important predictor of electability, and if young candidates are less likely than older ones to have held electoral office before becoming a candidate, then it is only logical that their representation is lower. In the average country of our CCS sample, about 70 percent of MPs keep their seat from one election to the next (see also Ansolabehere and Snyder 2002). In such a setting, it is very difficult for young candidates to be placed in an electable list position or nominated for a competitive or safe seat in a majoritarian system.

To break this incumbency advantage, we can think of at least three ways to render parliaments more accessible for the young. First, *term limits*, which we see as a legal restriction that limits the number of terms an officeholder may serve in a particular elected office, could make the recruitment process more open for the young. They would force parties to renew their representatives after a certain time. Second, the aforementioned youth quota regulations, if applied more stringently and on a larger scale, could help break this advantage of incumbents and offer youth better chances of winning a seat. A third solution could be that senior candidates *voluntarily step aside* and leave their spot to newcomers. Because this third solution is inherently implausible when it comes to people that seek influence, we deem this option as unlikely as the first two solutions. The first solution of term limits is a result of institutional reform, which empirically is not very common for national legislatures, so far. Today, countries such as Bolivia, Costa Rica, and the Philippines have such policies in place. Others, such as Ecuador, Mexico, and Venezuela have had such rules in the past but have discarded them through constitutional reform. In a further category of countries—including France, Peru, and Switzerland—term limits have been the subject of debate, but these debates have not yet translated into policy (see Republic of the Philippines 1987; Carey 1998; Schwindt-Bayer 2005; Council of Europe 2019). The second solution, or the adoption of (mandatory legislative) quota regulations, might be a fast track to render parliaments more representative in terms of age. Looking at the candidate data in our sample dataset, we can conclude that there would definitely not be any supply issue in filling these seats. However, what is missing is the societal demand for such measures, as well as parties' and legislators' willingness to adopt such measures. At this time, there is just no political will to implement these quotas in most countries.

Until parties are ready to actively push young candidates and place them more frequently into eligible positions, we deem it very unlikely that the current nomination pattern will change. Therefore we expect parties to continue to nominate young candidates in lower nonelectable list positions and, in majoritarian systems, to districts that the party has difficulty winning.

From the example of Switzerland, we also have preliminary evidence that younger candidates are disadvantaged at the election booth. Yet we do not know for sure who drives this preference for older candidates. We know from the voting literature that senior citizens vote more, as turnout more or less increases with age. If then senior citizens have a preference to vote for older candidates (in systems where they have the chance to do so), then we could explain at least part of the electoral advantage from which older candidates benefit. However, we need future research to confirm this conjecture.

On the more positive side, the example of Sweden suggests that young candidates are sometimes at an advantage. In Sweden, parties give young candidates a fair chance of winning a seat (by, for example, putting them in eligible list positions). It is also likely that young voters, as well as older voters, actively choose younger candidates' names on ballot lists. Both processes might feed into a positive feedback loop. More specifically, survey data from the ESS reveals that the political interest among youth in Sweden is significantly higher than the political interest among Swiss youth, where young candidates' chances of winning an election are among the lowest. This illustrative example suggests that in those societies that give young adults a fair chance to shape the political landscape, youth as a group show higher political interest. Consequently, the vicious cycle of political alienation might not be as pronounced in Sweden as it is in Switzerland.

CHAPTER 7

EXPLAINING (MORE) VARIATION IN YOUTH
REPRESENTATION

Insights from an Original Survey in Sweden
and Switzerland

It's best to have plenty of younger politicians in the mix: It's only from a
multiplicity of perspectives that some problems—and some solutions—
come clearly in to view. And older generations need younger ones to
reconnect them with their idealism.

(BRUNI 2019)

7.1. Added Value of an Original Survey with MPs and Candidates in
Sweden and Switzerland

In the quote above, there is a sentiment that we believe has value. If not
youth, then who else should bring new ideas to parliament? However, there
is a lot of wasted energy and innovation considering that the presence of
young adults in legislatures and cabinets is insufficient in most countries. In
the previous chapters, we have identified several country- and party-level
factors that contribute to youths' underrepresentation in parliaments and
cabinets. On the national level, age requirements above 18 years to run for
office and majoritarian electoral systems inhibit youths' access to parliament. On the party level, factors such as old party leaders and old parties—
and to some extent right-wing parties—tend to give rise to older parliamentary delegations. Moreover, for the cabinet, it is youths' parliamentary
representation and the age of the head of the government that matter, with
older legislatures and older heads of government triggering cabinets composed by older members.

The party- and country-level factors explain some of the variation in
youth representation across countries, but certainly not all variation. The
comparison in the previous chapter between unsuccessful and successful candidates in various countries illustrates another phenomenon: some

countries have high percentages of young adults on candidate lists or as district candidates, but very few of them tend to win a seat in the legislature. Other countries have comparatively few young candidates but a high share of young legislators. The two countries that stick out in this regard in the CCS are Sweden and Switzerland (see chapter 6). The CCS sample highlights that in the Swedish 2014 election, 21.37 percent of the candidates were 35 years or younger. Yet the percentage of elected MPs in this age cohort stood at 27.20 percent, the highest number in all countries in this sample. The actual numbers from 2018 (the most recent national election at the time of writing) confirm this high youth representation. In 2018, 22.6 percent of members of the Swedish Parliament were 35 years old or younger at the time of its constitution. This percentage is comparatively high, even if it falls short of the 29 percent that this age group amasses as a share of the voting-age population. However, the presence of the age group 40 years or under at 35.5 percent of MPs closely matches this group's representation within the voting-age population (albeit only at the beginning of the parliament).

The situation is different in Switzerland. The Swiss sample in the CCS, which refers to the 2015 election to the national parliament, has a very high share of young candidates (i.e., 43.96 percent of candidates in this survey were aged 35 years or under).[1] This high percentage of candidates is in contrast with the very low share of young adults that won a seat in the National Council; a mere 10.2 percent of those that won a seat were 35 years or under at the time of election.[2] When it comes to representation of this group, very little has changed for the 2019 parliament. The share of legislators aged 35 years or under at the formation of the parliament was 10.6 percent. This compares to the 28.1 percent that this age group constitutes in the Swiss voting-age population. This finding further implies that the underrepresentation is nearly one to three at the beginning of the 2019 legislature and lower than one to three at the end of the term. What slightly changed in Switzerland in the 2019 elections was the median and mean age. The median and mean age dropped by about one year from approximately 51 to 50 years for the former and approximately 50 years to 49 years for the latter measure.

---

1. The percentage of youth aged 35 or under who answered the questionnaire seem to reflect roughly the age distribution among candidates in Switzerland for this election. Data for the 2015 elections shows that about 34 percent of candidates were 30 years or under, pointing to the myriad of young adults running for office (Kohler and Tognina 2019).

2. We focus on the lower house of the Federal Assembly of Switzerland, The National Council, known as the Nationalrat (German), Conseil national (French), Consiglio nazionale (Italian), or Cussegl naziunal (Romansh).

The share of representatives aged 40 years or under increased, from roughly 23 percent to 25 percent (an age group that amasses 37 percent of the voting-age population).

In this chapter, we want to shed more light on this puzzle: why do young adults in Sweden have a higher likelihood of winning a seat, whereas young candidates in Switzerland still face strong sidelining? By highlighting this issue, we hope to gain additional insight into the factors that explain variation in youth representation across countries. Expressed differently, we aim to understand further nuances related to age-based discrimination. To meet this goal, we designed a short original survey consisting of five questions that we sent to candidates of the previous national elections and current MPs in Switzerland and Sweden. In the survey, we were interested in candidates' and elected MPs' perceptions of youth discrimination.

7.2. Methods

To gauge the perceptions of MPs and candidates, we designed a survey with questions that allowed for longer full-text answers. The survey had five themes, asking respondents the following questions: 1) Do you think that the age distribution in parliament should roughly correspond to the age distribution in the population? 2) In your opinion, is one age group systematically disadvantaged in the nomination of candidates? 3) Have you witnessed age-related disadvantages in nominations? If so, please explain. 4) In your opinion, should there be a higher share of young MPs in the national legislature? 5) What should parties do so that more young people run and become elected? We also recorded information such as respondents' present position, age, gender, and party affiliation.

We sent our questionnaire through email to all MPs in Sweden and Switzerland in January 2020.[3] We found all email addresses on the respective national parliamentary website. For candidates, we sampled only from those running for the most recent national election (i.e., 2018 in Sweden and 2019 in Switzerland). However, finding the contact information for candidates was more difficult. While there are public lists of those who ran in the elections in the two countries, these lists are very long and do not provide email addresses. We used these lists as a basis and engaged in a process of several

---

3. In Sweden, we posed these questions in Swedish. For Switzerland we opted for both a French and a German version.

steps to sample candidates. First, we limited our search to political parties represented in the two respective parliaments and focused on the inventory of all candidates that ran for those parties. For the Swedish case, we tried to identify as many email addresses as possible. Generally, we searched those persons on higher list positions earlier, as it was easier to find their email addresses, aiming to contact at least 50 candidates per party. Some parties also use the relatively simple approach of giving candidates a "name.sur-name@partyname.se" address. This made it relatively easy for us to reach out to candidates in these parties, despite the fact that some of these emails bounced back. In total, we contacted about 1,000 candidates (in addition to the 349 MPs).

For Switzerland, we contacted party offices and asked them to distribute our survey to their candidates. Three parties replied in the affirmative and sent out our queries to all of their candidates in one canton. For the other parties, we spent some considerable time searching for email addresses. We found the candidates' contact information primarily through party websites, personal websites, and searches in records available on the Internet. In total, we managed to contact around 500 candidates in Switzerland (in addition to the 200 MPs).

We could derive a large sample from both settings, albeit a larger one for Sweden (see table 27). In Sweden, 399 politicians participated in our survey (120 MPs and 279 candidates). In particular, we deem the response rate of 34.44 percent among Swedish MPs to be high. From the approximately 1,000 candidates we contacted, 279 responded, which translates into a respectable response rate of about 28 percent. Concerning the average and median age (as well as the share of men and women), our pool of participating Swedish MPs resembles the population of MPs in parliament quite well. For candidates, we also have a very diverse sample (see table 27). For Switzerland, our sample was much smaller. In total, 106 candidates and MPs participated. The response rate was also much lower, particularly among MPs. Only 12 percent of the members of the National Council sent our questionnaire back. Contrary to Sweden, we also have an overrepresentation of young politicians in the MP pool of respondents, but not in the candidate pool.

Despite the fact that we cannot treat the answers to our survey as representative of all legislators and candidates, we nevertheless provide some summary statistics for the first four of our five questions. This accounts for an overview of the answers we received. To do so, we coded individual answers into two categories (people who answered in the affirmative and people who voiced their disapproval). To calculate our descriptive statistics,

Table 27. Descriptive statistics of our sample of MPs and candidates in Sweden and Switzerland

	All MPs	MPs aged 40 years or under	All candidates	Candidates aged 40 years or under
Sweden				
N	120	37	279	85
Share 35 or under (in %)	19.17	62.16	22.58	74.12
Share 40 or under (in %)	31.66	100	30.47	100
Mean age	47.79	33.08	49.22	30.96
Median age	48.50	33.00	49.00	30.00
Share women (in %)	50.83	51.35	49.29	40
Switzerland				
N	24	7	82	39
Share 35 or under (in %)	25.00	85.71	43.90	92.31
Share 40 or under (in %)	19.14	100	48.78	100
Mean age	48.54	31.29	42.46	26.64
Median age	50.00	32.00	46.00	25.00
Share women (in %)	37.50	71.43	52.44	58.97

we assigned the value of 1 for affirmative answers and the value of 0 for disapproving answers. Most of the time, this coding was simple. To illustrate, respondents generally answered the first question—on whether parliaments should reflect the age distribution in the population—with either "yes" or "no" and then some text to justify their answer. There were only a few tough cases. We found similar trends in questions two to four.

The summary statistics for the four questions give us some broad-based idea of respondents' perception about contemporary levels of youth representation. For example, these trends allow us to decipher to what extent respondents in Switzerland see youth as underrepresented, if they find this underrepresentation (un)justified, and if they think that politics should change course to render the system more accommodating for youth. In contrast, for Sweden, these broader strokes help us gauge whether there is a general political culture favoring youth, whether respondents are satisfied that youths' share in parliament comes close to their share in the population, or whether there is some hesitation in having youth represented in such high numbers in the national parliament.

After these more general discussions of the results in our two countries, we engage in an in-depth analysis of the qualitative answers to questions one to four, aiming to explain the differences in representation. The final part of the chapter evaluates question five, aiming to identify additional factors that could help increase the parliamentary representation of young adults. In particular, we look at some additional insights that go beyond the factors identified in the previous chapters, and we especially try to identify what parties could do to further support young candidates.

7.3. Quantitative and Qualitative Insights of Our Survey

7.3.1. Should There Be a Correspondence in the Age Structure of Parliaments and Populations?

To begin the survey, we asked respondents whether the age structure of parliament should correspond to the age structure in the population. A majority of both the Swedish and the Swiss samples answer in the affirmative (see table 28). Yet what is quite surprising is that there are more affirmative answers in Switzerland than in Sweden. We can only speculate about the reasons for this unexpected finding. Possibly there is a higher urgency in Switzerland, where only slightly more than 10 percent of contemporary MPs were 35 years or younger at the inception of the 2019 parliament.

In Sweden, though a majority still suggests that a balanced age representation is important, not everyone might be happy with the fact that the Swedish parliament is "younger" than many other parliaments elsewhere in Europe and across the world. In particular, there are some strong voices against the relatively high presence of elected young adults, mainly among elderly politicians. A male candidate aged 70 is such a strong voice. He states:

> Young people are quite often radical and often lack "realism," which could be both good and bad: It could be good in parties because they are catalysts and creators of ideas, but bad for decision making, where they should not have too much influence.

Another illustrating example of a more critical view on having many young politicians is the views of this male MP, aged 61 years:

> You cannot expect to end up in the Riksdag until you have experience of how society works. Parliamentarians should have experience and knowledge of leadership and preferably in some professional area. This does not

exclude young members, but I believe that this means that this group should be less represented in Parliament.

Of course, we must note that these (older) politicians made these statements in a setting of relatively high youth representation (which is, however, still below the share of youth in the voting-age population). Nevertheless, they illustrate that the election of a high share of relatively young politicians does not find the support of everyone. According to background information that some of the respondents provided, the trend of relatively high youth representation is a recent feature of the past 15 years. This also implies that the gains youth have made in terms of representation are still fragile. There were also indications from a handful of accounts that youth representation at the local and regional level is much lower than at the national level.

Yet we should not assume that everyone who disagrees with the view that the age distribution in the Riksdag should reflect the Swedish population favor a higher share of older legislators. Table 28 highlights another interesting feature: it is young MPs and, even more so, young candidates who do not agree with the view that the age structure in parliament should reflect the age structure in society. In theory, young politicians could favor an overrepresentation of older legislators or an overrepresentation of younger legislators. As a general rule, however, youth do not mention the possibility of an overrepresentation of older MPs in the more qualitative answers. In fact, if they mention anything, these younger respondents believe that there should be an overrepresentation of young politicians. As some of our respondents either explicitly or implicitly mention, the perspective that young politicians must live the longest with the laws that present parliaments decide upon now could justify this point of view.

In contrast, in Switzerland most of our respondents—regardless of whether they are candidates or elected MPs—are in favor of having the age distribution in parliament reflect the population. The affirmative answers range from an absolute necessity to have youth represented according to their age structure in society to answers stating that such an equal representation would be preferable. Young respondents particularly articulate this strive to gain adequate representation. This support is logical given that legislators under 40, and even more so under 35, are strongly disadvantaged in the Swiss National Council. However, as in Sweden, there are also some forthright voices *against* a principle of reflecting the population's age distribution in the legislature. A 64-year-old female MP describes her opposition to this view as follows:

Table 28. Distribution of answers to the question whether the age distribution in parliament should correspond to the age distribution in the general population

	All MPs	MPs aged 40 years or under	All candidates	Candidates aged 40 years or under
Sweden				
Number of observations	120	37	279	85
Yes answers (in %)	65.83	67.57	58.78	45.88
No answers (in %)	30	32.43	41.22	52.92
N/A answers (in %)	4.17	0	0	1.18
Switzerland				
Number of observations	24	7	82	39
Yes answers (in %)	72.92	100	62.20	82.05
No answers (in %)	27.18	0	27.80	17.95
N/A answers (in %)	0	0	0	0

You need to acquire the necessary personal and professional experience and network connections to be an efficient parliamentarian. These skills come with seniority. Therefore, it is correct that legislators are older than the average working population.

Another respondent, a 66-year-old female candidate, puts it even more drastically:

Politics is no picnic: It is hard work. Youth should not complain, they should work hard to be elected, because it is even more work once you are elected.

7.3.2. Are There Systematic Disadvantages of One Age Group in the Nomination of Candidates to the Two Parliaments?

The second question, whether respondents think that any particular age group faces disadvantages in elections to the two contemporary parliaments, offers some very interesting observations. In Sweden, if anything, there is a moderate consensus among respondents that it is older people who are disadvantaged in nominations (see table 29). This finding is still somewhat surprising, considering that youth are not overrepresented if we compare their share in parliament with their share in the Swedish voting-age population. Of course, it is true that, comparatively, Sweden has a relatively young parliament: the mean and median age of parliamentarians were roughly 45 years when the parliament formed in 2018. Yet the percentage of legislators aged 35 years or under, which is 22.6 percent, falls short of the 29 percent that this cohort amasses among voting age citizens. For our second measure, legislators aged 40 years or under, there is only some slight under-representation in the share of youth in the population compared to youth in society; youth in parliament roughly make up 35.5 percent of the members, compared to 37 percent in the Swedish voting-age population. However, these numbers also imply that at the end of the current parliament—in the year 2022—there will also be a larger age gap. Hence we cannot speak of an overrepresentation of youth. We must keep this in mind when we interpret the answers from Sweden. Nonetheless, it is also true that people above 60 years old face some underrepresentation compared to the other age groups in the Riksdag. Those aged 60 and above at the beginning of the 2019 parliament constituted slightly more than 7 percent of parliamentarians (in 2022 the number will be higher) but a full 27 percent in the voting-age population. However, if we look only at the full-time working population above 60, the 7 percent parliamentary representation is slightly above the full-time working population. According to Larson and Pederson (2017), the percentage of full-time employees is roughly 20 percent of the age group 61 to 69 and negligibly small beyond 70. While we do not want to get into a discussion about whether parliament should resemble the working age population or the eligible voting population, we can nevertheless maintain that the presence of the middle-aged in Sweden comes at the expense of both young and older age groups. Interestingly, in the qualitative answers, hardly anybody mentions that the presence of middle-aged representatives should decrease. Instead the old respondents rather seem to point to a high presence of young MPs as being the problem.

In Switzerland, a majority of the responding senior candidates and MPs answered that there are no systematic disadvantages of any age group, including youth. We find this tendency remarkable, given that the group of people aged 35 years or under have a representation ratio of one to three in the National Council compared to their share in the voting-age population. We see three possible scenarios that could explain discrepancies between survey answers and the empirical reality: (1) survey respondents do not see youths' underrepresentation as a problem. However, if this is the case, they should not have answered in the affirmative for our first question on whether or not the age representation in parliament should reflect the age representation in society. (2) They have insufficient knowledge of the age of their colleagues. We find this possibility also relatively unlikely to apply

Table 29. Answers to the question whether any age group is systematically disadvantaged

	All MPs	MPs aged 40 years or under	All candidates	Candidates aged 40 years or under
Sweden				
Number of observations	120	37	279	85
Older respondents are underrepresented (in %)	50.83	45.96	34.41	31.76
Younger MPs are underrepresented (in %)	2.50	2.70	10.75	11.76
Both younger and older MPs are underrepresented (in %)	15.83	24.32	18.64	1.18
Middle-aged MPs are underrepresented (in %)	0.83	0	3.94	0
Middle-aged and older MPs are underrepresented (in %)	2.5	0	2.73	1.18
No one is underrepresented (in %)	13.33	16.21	29.03	29.41
No answer (percent)	14.83	10.81	3.58	1.18
Switzerland				
Number of observations	24	7	82	39
Older respondents are underrepresented (in %)	0	0	6.10	0
Younger MPs are underrepresented (in %)	33.34	57.14	32.93	56.41
Both younger and older MPs are underrepresented (in %)	4.17	0	7.32	7.69
Middle-aged MPs are underrepresented (in %)	0	0	1.22	2.56
Middle-aged and older MPs are underrepresented (in %)	0	0	0	0
No one is underrepresented (in %)	62.50	42.86	52.44	33.33
No answer (percent)	0	0	0	0

given that older MPs work with younger ones on a daily basis. (3) They know that there is some age-based disadvantage in elections but do not want to act on it. We deem this third option the most likely.

Answers from MPs such as "no there is no systematic disadvantage because youth can run on the youth lists" manifest the tendency that older MPs and candidates seem to use explanations for the lack of youth in the National Council that do not hold up to scrutiny. Rather than being random, some structural problems disadvantage the election of youth. Most pronounced of these problems is the parties' possibility to have so-called secondary or annex lists alongside the main list. That is, organized groups within the party, such as the youth wing, the business wing, or the pensioners' wing, can run their own lists, so-called *sister lists*. This happens frequently to youth wings of the main parties. Rather than being placed on the main party's list, the mother party encourages the youth wing to present its own list. In the 2019 general elections, there were youth lists in most cantons for the main parties. Yet, according to one male candidate aged 22, these youth lists are "the devil in disguise." These lists allow the mother party to relegate all or most young adults from the main list to the secondary list under the pretext that the party's youth wing has its own list. These youth lists generally do not get enough votes to send anybody to Bern. Having separate youth lists would not be a problem if youth were to get a fair share on the main lists. In such a scenario, youth on these lists could gain some experience campaigning and can be active as agenda setters. However, this institutional feature becomes problematic if party elites do not recognize that youth lists—without any mechanism to place youth on the main list as well—actually hinder young politicians' ability to gain a seat in the National Council. Therefore respondents who put forward the answer that youth have their own lists where they can seek nomination seem to neglect that youth lists do not allow young adults to gain representation. Rather these youth lists contribute to the age-based discrimination against youth, making it harder for young adults to win a parliamentary seat in Switzerland.

Another answer we see as somewhat dodging the problem is the response: "we as a party would have liked to put more young candidates on the main party list. Unfortunately, we did not find suitable candidates." This reference to a small supply of candidates just does not stand up to any empirical testing. To us, this answer also looks more like an expedient answer, especially taking into account that Switzerland has among the youngest candidates of Western countries (see chapter 6). If there are enough young candidates to fill a whole youth list in a canton, there will definitely be enough to exchange their place on the youth list for a spot on the main party list.

In contrast to their senior colleagues, who frequently seem to dodge the problem, a majority of young MPs and candidates acknowledge that there are some systematic disadvantages for young politicians. Among other things, these young respondents point toward a political culture of seniority, the difficulty—if not impossibility—of young candidates to make it on main party lists, and the necessity to have prior electoral experience at the local or cantonal level. In addition, several young candidates mention an additional feature of these aforementioned youth lists: these lists seem to be rather independent from the main list. While this independence allows youth to campaign for themselves—and push their beliefs, such as those related to the problem of climate change—these loose connections to the main list seem to inhibit youth from figuring prominently on the main list.

7.3.3. Have Respondents Witnessed Any Age-Based Discrimination in Nominations?

The answers to this third question show further nuance between the two countries (see table 30). In Sweden, a larger share of respondents indicated that they have witnessed age-based discrimination than in Switzerland. At first glance, this result seems surprising given the rather strong record of youth representation in parliament. However, if we consider that we have a significant amount of old survey participants in Sweden, who affirm that they themselves have witnessed aged-based discrimination, the higher numbers for Sweden make more sense. In this Nordic country, accounts of such a disadvantage come from both young and old respondents. Youth mention obstacles of different kinds to get a seat. For example, a 34-year-old male MP explains:

> The political parties are closed societies—imagine a Rotary Association nowadays. People who apply for nominations can be of all different ages, but those who get the chance are the ones who are members for a long time and who know the unwritten rules.

Another MP, aged 36, puts the subtle disadvantages youth still face as follows:

> There is no outright discrimination, but more of a structural problem . . . because of the seniority principle, members with the longest service and maximum age will receive the most benefits.

Young politicians, in the grand majority, advance the argument that there might be some disadvantage for young people gaining nominations or elected seats. An unsuccessful 63-year-old female candidate is one of the few examples of an older politician who advances the argument that youth still face hurdles, referring to a culture of seniority in political parties that youth have difficulty overcoming. She explains this culture as follows: "In my own party there are many older people who find it difficult to let go and give way to the younger ones." However, this older woman remains the exception of a senior respondent suggesting that youth face difficulties to gain a seat in the national parliament. In contrast to young respondents, older respondents in the sample generally suggest that it is instead older politicians who face obstacles. An unsuccessful 57-year-old candidate explains:

> The age discrimination I find most noticeable is that many older people fall out of the line in favor of young people. And that may be good, but as our former party leader put it: "Age is not a disease." In Sweden, we are poor at taking advantage of the elderly's experience.

Another senior male MP proposes a similar argument:

> Older people are definitely disadvantaged in all respects nowadays, and I would say even middle-aged. There is a huge belief that young people without life experience and work experience can become good politicians. Not infrequently, this belief proves wrong. I find it weird that young people without experience, education and knowledge are entrusted with heavy management tasks that they would never receive in business or the public sector.

In Switzerland, fewer respondents share experiences of age-based discrimination, either personally or within their party. It is telling that the highest percentage of those having personally experienced any age-based discrimination comes from the group of unsuccessful candidates aged 40 years or under. Representative of this group is the response from a 35-year-old female candidate, who describes the discrimination she had to endure as follows:

> I put forward my candidacy for the national parliament a couple of years ago. My nomination was doomed to fail. The party leadership told me that as a young woman I would suffer from massive attacks from other candidates. For that reason, they discouraged me from running.

Other answers mention that eligible list positions on the cantonal list are almost exclusively reserved for older candidates. While most of those references to age-based discrimination come from young candidates or MPs, there are senior politicians who acknowledge that youth face hurdles, but these voices remain a minority. For example, some respondents acknowledge that youth lists never get enough votes to send somebody to the National Council. Yet none of these older politicians is as vocal as young respondents. "It is a trap for young politicians to be placed on a youth list."

Table 30. Answers to the question whether the respondent has witnessed any age-based discrimination

	All MPs	MPs 40 or under	All candidates	Candidates 40 or under
Sweden				
Number of observations	120	37	279	85
Yes, has witnessed discrimination (in %)	30.00	35.14	40.14	41.18
No, has not witnessed discrimination (in %)	56.67	45.95	56.99	57.65
No answer (in %)	13.33	18.92	2.87	1.18
Sweden				
Number of observations	24	7	81	39
Yes, has witnessed discrimination (in %)	17.39	16.67	24.67	32.89
No, has not witnessed discrimination (in %)	82.61	83.33	75.33	67.11
No answer (in %)	0	0	0	0

This quote from a 32-year-old candidate summarizes the feeling of some youth candidates quite well. It seems that the installation of youth lists allows youth to run, but it also allows the mainstream parties to keep youth largely absent from their main list. Given that the electoral rule in Switzerland links these side lists to the main list, they help the mother party gain more votes. However, they do not help individuals on the youth party list gain a seat. Other groups within the party, such as pensioners, sometimes also have their own lists, but these groups also figure more prominently on the main list.

Of course, the failure of youth lists to generate any MPs is also a problem of the electorate. In theory, voters could vote for these "secondary" lists, but they hardly ever do so. By voting for these lists, Swiss voters might also risk "wasting" their vote, because not a sufficiently high number of other voters cast such votes.

7.3.4. Should There Be a Larger Number of Young MPs?

Among candidates and MPs in Sweden, the distribution between those who think that there should be a larger number of young MPs and those opposing this proposition is about 40 percent compared to roughly 50 percent (see table 31). Looking at the full-text responses, we can discern some inter-

Table 31. Answers to the question whether there should be a higher number of young MPs in the national parliament

	All MPs	MPs 40 or under	All candidates	Candidates 40 or under
Sweden				
N	120	37	279	85
Yes, there should be more young MPs (in %)	37.50	54.05	44.09	42.35
No, there should not be more young MPs (in %)	53.85	32.43	54.12	56.47
No answer (in %)	21.76	13.51	1.79	1.18
Switzerland				
N	24	7	82	39
Yes, there should be more young MPs (in %)	58.33	57.14	73.78	92.31
No, there should not be more young MPs (in %)	41.67	42.86	26.22	7.69
No answer (in %)	0	0	0	0

esting patterns and nuances: those who do not necessarily think that more young legislators should access the national legislature are split between satisfaction with current levels and demanding more politicians that are older. One 75-year-old male candidate explains this satisfaction as follows: "It is good as it is. The playing field is even. Equal to everyone." Others, such as a 57-year-old male candidate, advocate for an increased share of older representatives. He states:

> In Sweden, we are poor at taking advantage of the elderly's experience. This is a big difference to dominant views in Europe and the rest of the world. There you can get the right confidence at 75, while here you are considered completely consumed.

A female MP aged 54 adds that "young people always receive a lot of attention. It is a bigger problem that we lack representation from the age of 65–80." Similarly, a 63-year-old candidate describes how perceptions of a youth advantage has led to big protests among older members of her party; according to her, this even led to an exit of older politicians.

These views are in contrast to the approximately 40 percent of respondents who think that there should be more young adults in the Swedish parliament. Most of these study subjects add that increases in youth representation are even more important in assemblies outside the Riksdag. We can broadly divide the statements that this second group advances into two main arguments. First, several respondents make the point that youth still lack influential positions inside and outside the parliament. For example, a female MP aged 45 years notes that "among the board members and in the party associations, there is an excess of the elderly." Respondents in this group also identify the problem of supply of competent young candidates. According to a 61-year-old male candidate, it is problematic if we only look at those currently elected. In his words:

> I think the question [of the age distribution among MPs] is wrong. The question that should be asked is—do we lack young local politicians? If this is the case, it could mean that we are heading towards a shortage of future competent parliamentary politicians.

In addition, it appears from quite a few answers that municipal politics is mainly recreational politics, which not only demands a lot of time but is also dominated by older persons. A 49-year-old female MP summarizes this view:

> As a member of parliament, you can live comfortably. Such a job provides good pay and opportunities to pursue other things within the party. It is a real job and a career for young people. You can spend a lot of time on political assignments in a municipality, but at the expense of your spare time. For a municipal council assignment, only a few hundred dollars a month are available. Then you should read documents, attend group meetings, be responsible for a portfolio and otherwise be active in the party. Therefore, it is mostly pensioners in municipal policy. Those who have time for it. We have few counselors in their thirties and forties in municipal politics.

A final theme among Swedish respondents is a reflection on the type of young candidates who win a seat. A 34-year-old male MP expresses this viewpoint as follows: "There is absolutely no need for more young politicians who joined a party when they were teenagers—however, more young politicians who have not been raised in youth wings are needed, especially from the suburbs of big cities."

In Switzerland, a majority of respondents supports an increase of youth representatives in the National Council (see table 31). However, most of these positive answers frequently still maintain that there is no systematic disadvantage to youth. The wish to see the number of young adults increase is particularly high for candidates and especially so among young candidates. More than 90 percent of the candidates in our Swiss sample favor an increase of youth in the national legislature. In general, young respondents, but also more senior ones, mention aspects such as generational justice, the fact that young candidates bring new ideas, and that solutions to problems such as climate change need fresh perspectives. For example, a 25-year-old female candidate justifies the need for a higher share of young representatives as follows:

> Let us talk about climate change. The older generations, who are in the majority in parliament now, are relatively little affected by this crisis. This is different for the younger generation. This dominance of the elderly in the national parliament has considerable effects on the formulation of laws; it affects if anything will be done.

We could also read some frustration in several comments from young candidates surrounding the question of whether youth should gain more representation. These voices point out that they wish for improvements in young adults' representation in the national parliament. At the same time, most respondents are hesitant to believe that things will change, at least in the short term. For example, young respondents point out that it is nerve-wracking to organize party lists and campaigns without any chances of winning. Through such activities, they manage to get some public attention, despite not having a real chance of gaining a seat in Bern. Nevertheless, these youth feel the frustration of their sidelining. At the same time, they express passion. For example, some young candidates mention that participating in the election allowed them to raise some more awareness of topics such as climate change or migration. A 21-year-old female candidate expresses this idealism as follows:

> We knew it beforehand that it was impossible for us to gain a seat. Therefore, we campaigned to gain media attention, influence the public discourse and attract more members for your youth party.

However, far from all candidates and MPs in the Swiss sample agree with the premise that youth should get higher representation. There is a diversity of responses, with respondents proposing three types of views. A first set of answers noted that youth representation is not an issue of importance. For instance, a 66-year-old male candidate sees age as "irrelevant" for being a good politician. A second cluster points toward the aforementioned lack of experience as a criterion for why there should not be more youth. A third group simply states that the parties decide upon nominations and one should not intervene in this process.

7.4. Youth in the Swedish Riksdag: Some Positive Signs but Still a Long Way to Full Acceptance

There have been many positive signs of improvements in youth representation in Sweden over the past decades. Youths' presence in the Riksdag has increased since the late 1990s to a respectable 22.6 percent for the cohort of adults aged 35 years or under. The share of those aged 40 years or under (measured at the time of the election) increased to an even more respectable 35.5 percent. Many respondents' perceptions confirm such improvements, not only in terms of numerical presence but also in the political culture of the country. For example, a 37-year-old female MP concludes: "As a rule, young people have been disadvantaged, but things have gotten better." Another female MP, aged 32, adds: "When I was younger, I was often told that I was inexperienced, and should therefore 'wait for my turn.' I feel that this kind of reasoning is generally less common today."

It seems that at least two features have favored this increase in youth representation. First, parties have set in place informal procedures that support young individuals. For example, one female respondent reports that her party has informal standards for the composition of lists, which state that candidates should reflect the population as much as possible. In addition, nominating committees should make special efforts to reach underrepresented groups. Several other politicians note that the specific party they belong to, the Social Democratic Party, has the goal that one-fourth of all candidates on a list should be aged 35 years or under. This scheme was formally anchored at the 2009 Congress by the party's membership; it approved a motion put forward by this party's influential youth organization (see Hennel 2010), but it is not technically a quota scheme with functioning sanctions. Yet our responses mention that this principle guides the party's nominations.

Second, youth wings of political parties seem to be a strong force to push young candidacies; they help socialize youth into politics and play an important role in recruiting candidates. Several of our survey respondents further mention that youth wings have considerable influence within the mother party; they often succeed in placing youth on eligible positions on party lists. In the words of a female MP, aged 61: "Strong local youth associations join together to vote for their young candidates. Older people rarely have similarly organized support."

However, not everyone supports this push to render politics more accessible to young adults. Changes in formal and informal rules have certainly improved the standing of youth. At the same time, however, these changes have also increased tensions between younger and older members and might have alienated some more senior politicians from the political system. A 34-year-old female MP explains these changing perceptions in the following words:

> In the last two decades the larger political discourse in Sweden has clearly sought to include young people in politics in different ways, in order to reach the "voices of the future." It has probably meant that in many places, many young people have come forward that the elderly have taken a step back, either by themselves or because they have felt "forced" to do so.

Our survey responses also offer ample evidence that some elderly politicians do not want to step aside. For example, there are respondents who think that the ideal age for an MP is 75 years, or who perceive it as problematic that the age group between 65 to 80 years has a relatively low political presence. From many responses, we also noticed some subtle—and sometimes not so subtle—resentment of youth. To illustrate, we have plenty of accounts in our responses that link youths' lack of experience to their ability to carry out their responsibilities. For example, a 23-year-old female MP tells us that middle-aged and older people repeatedly expressed to her that young people such as herself should not be taken seriously in politics as they "lack life experience" and are "too young and immature." Another female MP, aged 48, adds that that there is still an underlying political culture in Sweden that youth lack the life experience needed to understand politics, society, and everyday life. A 66-year-old candidate brings this objection of youths' capability to govern to the point. For him, experience and youth are an "impossible combination."

Another related recurring theme from the survey is that young candidates and politicians do not face the same standards as their more senior colleagues. Instead our data point to plenty of examples of condescending comments by older politicians directed against younger ones. For example, a male candidate, aged 20, who serves on his town's municipal council, reports that belittling behavior toward young people is quite common:

> To take my own example, I was given a municipal trust assignment when I was 18, but representatives of other parties addressed me with 'kid' and 'boy' instead of my name, during meetings.

A 31-year-old female MP states that during her tenure in the municipal council, she heard politicians expressing opinions such as, "is she not too young to be able to sit in the municipal council?" Another MP, a woman of 43 years, further illustrate these attitudes:

> There are plenty of master suppression techniques and I have witnessed more than once that older politicians act derogatory towards younger politicians and use their age against them.

Finally, a 23-year-old candidate explains in his response that others voice oppositions toward his views by questioning his personality and that age is a primary factor in these attacks against him.

We can interpret these experiences of young politicians, but also of not-so-young ones, as warning signs. Despite Sweden being one of the countries in the world with the highest share of youth in the national parliament, young adults still do not seem to meet a level playing field in Swedish politics. Our understanding is that the gains that youth have made in the past years are still fragile, even more so because many of the survey participants point toward a different situation at the municipal level, where older politicians are present in higher numbers. Data from the Swedish statistical authority bolster these claims. In municipal councils, young adults are present to a lower degree than their share of the general population (SCB 2020).[4] Moreover, these data also suggest that young council members are less likely to stay in such positions once elected. An analysis of people that left their municipal council seat in between 2014 and 2018 demonstrates that young people are much more likely than other age groups to exit their assignment before completing their term.[5] More than 40 percent of munic-

---

4. As stated in a report by Statistics Sweden: "Young people, aged 18–29, are under-represented compared to the population. They make up 7 percent of municipal politicians, which is 12 percentage points lower than the proportion in the voting-age population" (SCB 2020, 6).

5. It is outside the scope of our book to study why this is so. We note that the most ambi-

ipal councilors, who were under the age of 30 years, chose to exit their seat prematurely during this time span (SCB 2019). These premature exits might be related to the time commitment these municipal posts demand. Available research (Erlingsson and Öhrvall 2010) suggests that people in general who exit Swedish municipal-level office before the end of their appointment do so for mostly private reasons, in addition to political ones (see footnote 52). From our findings, it appears that young adults in such positions still face some opposition and belittling behaviors due to their age. Therefore we believe that describing Sweden as an exemplary "success case" in terms of youths' presence in politics risks shading processes inside councils and parliaments pointing toward a culture of superiority dominated by more senior politicians.

7.5. Youth in the Swiss National Council: Still the Exception Rather Than the Rule

The middle-aged and elderly still dominate Switzerland's National Council. To illustrate, the share of young MPs aged 35 years or under is still lower than the one of MPs above 61 years (10.6 percent versus 12.6 percent, respectively). This implies that at the end of the parliamentary term of the 2019 parliament, only 10.6 percent of legislators will be 40 years or under, but the share of those above 61 years will exceed 15 percent.

While a majority of respondents recognizes the low presence of young adults, from the responses we received we do not think that the majority wants to address the problem of youths' underrepresentation seriously. Several respondents also downplay the problem of youths' lack of presence in the National Council or point to so-called success stories. The comment of this middle-aged MP reflects such neglect of the problem: "In the last Swiss national elections many young people, in particular many young females, became newly elected MPs." Our impression is that such statements shy away from the fact that this group is underrepresented at a ratio

---

tious study on this topic that we could find, Erlingsson and Öhrvall (2010), confirms the finding that young people are more likely than other age groups to leave Swedish local politics before the end of their term. From the general pool of those leaving municipal elected office, it was more common to do so for "private" reasons (62 percent of respondents in a smaller sample of ex-politicians), rather than "political" reasons (25 percent). Thirteen percent sorted in the category "private and political reasons have an equally large importance" (p. 67).

of 1 to 3 relative to the population. Other statements, such as the one by this 66-year-old female candidate, illustrate that some politicians do not want to see the problem as such but rather try to find some justification, which does not acknowledge the lack of youth representation in Swiss national politics:

> If young adults want to get higher representation, they should get involved more, become a candidate and get elected. They should stop complaining that they have few chances. If youth really want to do something, they should increase their engagement. Complaining does not count for me.

We find it noteworthy that this view bases itself on some problematic assumptions, to say the least. From what we can tell, there is no lack of youth engagement. To illustrate, the share of candidates aged 30 years or under averaged around 10 percent in the 1970s and 1980s and increased to around 20 percent in the elections during the 1990s. It then witnessed another gradual increase: during the five elections since 2003, about 30 percent of all candidates to the National Council have been under 30 years of age. In fact, in the last three elections, the share of candidates in this age group exceeded 30 percent (Kohler and Tognina 2019). Confronted with these numbers, the suggestion of a lack of young candidates in Swiss politics does not hold water. As youth presence on youth lists reveals, young adults show a strong commitment to take an active part in electoral politics.

We believe that it is important that politicians start perceiving the lack of youth in parliament as a problem. Suggestions that there are not enough young candidates are clearly misleading. If there were no candidates, maybe this supply argument could make sense, but with record numbers of young candidates running there is objectively no dearth of youth willing to run. Rather middle-aged and senior candidates must recognize that the problem is structural. Most often, young candidates are relegated to side lists. This provides a double advantage for the more senior party elites; it allows them to add votes to the party (even if it is only 1 or 2 percent, or even less than 1 percent). In addition, it permits them to keep most of the list positions for themselves, without the need for an older candidate to step aside in favor of a younger candidate.

Youth can only see considerable improvements if young candidates make it to the main lists. It is important to note that we do not advocate for the abolition of youth lists. Being a candidate on a youth list can be a stepping-stone for a political career and can provide youth with some firsthand experience in running a campaign. In addition, these youth lists can help candidates gain media attention for topics important to young citizens. Yet if youth face near complete relegation to these lists, they will not win elections. We therefore recommend that the installation of a youth list should be coupled with some level of mandatory youth representation on the main list (targets could be 25 or 30 percent). Such permeability would not only open youth to some increased representation in the National Council but it would also show them that they are welcome on the main list. In fact, such a target or quota could also allow Swiss political parties to renew themselves periodically. As the example of the Social Democratic Party in Sweden reveals, quota or target measures can be important to improve the chances for young candidates.

In addition to the institutional feature of reforming such youth lists, it seems that there must be a strengthening of the societal consciousness in favor of higher youth representation. This brings us back to the aforementioned vicious cycle of political apathy. In the Swiss case, youths' political interest is low, to say the least: they are the age group that participates the least in elections, and—as we have shown here—their voices are largely absent in parliament. There are several ways to break this vicious cycle. For example, if society as a whole recognizes that youth are an integral part, they might grant them more representation. Another possibility would be stronger youth advocacy. Youth must wake up and demand their fair share of legislative seats and other influential posts. The youth climate strikes, which triggered strong mobilization in 2018 and 2019, point to a possible political awakening of youth. Yet it remains an open question how sustainable this activism is and whether it will lead to even more young adults running for office and possibly also more elected young MPs, as well as how society responds to these calls for change.

So far, the Swiss society—and the majority of countries on the globe for that matter—have failed to incorporate young adults into formal decision-making bodies. However, Swiss history provides a prominent example that the quite conservative political culture in this Alpine country can change. The development of women's elected presence has shown that society can rectify injustices in political influence. To highlight, Switzerland was one of the last countries with democratic institutions to enfranchise women at the national level. Until 1971, women had no right to run and stand for office in its federal assemblies. Yet women's parliamentary representation has increased strongly since women gained the right to vote and to run for office: from 5 percent in 1971 to more than 40 percent in 2019 (see Favero 2019). We could therefore hope for a similar increase in youth representation over the next years and decades. Most candidates and MPs recognize the dearth of youth representation as a problem. It would be a start if party elites were to act on this problem and start changing course, by actively promoting more young adults on the main party lists and, particularly, by pushing these young candidates through endorsements and favorable positions.

7.6. Propositions to Increase Youth Representation

Despite the fact that the state of youth representation differs in Sweden and Switzerland, the propositions that our survey respondents voiced to increase youth representation resemble each other, except for the specific case of the *youth lists* in Switzerland. For youth to become less of an exception in Swiss politics, it seems that there must be reform in the use of youth lists. The overall majority of young candidates runs on specific youth lists; youth run, campaign, and fight for their convictions, with no chance of getting elected. It is unlikely, to say the least, that they would not be willing to run on the party's main list. One suggestion could thus be to keep youth lists as a stepping-stone for a larger number of young candidates. At the same time, parties should be required to grant them a certain number of positions on the main lists.

Aside from this more specific point, all other topics apply to both settings and have general reach. *Regulating incumbency* is one recurring topic. For example, one Swedish female candidate, aged 23, suggests this type of reform:

> One possibility is that the party itself can begin to set limits on how many periods a parliamentary member may hold office. One problem that keeps many young people out is that once a person is elected, he can sit for 20 years. As a result, the flow becomes slow and entering as a new MP is then rather about running in the right election than being the best candidate. This affects all candidates so nothing is specific to young people, although such a measure will have a greater impact on us.

Similarly, a 53-year-old male candidate from Switzerland advocates term limits of 16 years. To us, this suggestion seems balanced. Being able to run four times would allow for some consistency, but it would also permit regular renewal. Other recurrent themes are *reducing the eligibility requirements* in various ways, such as lowering the right to vote and to run for office to

16 years, as well as introducing special mentor programs that pair young aspiring candidates with more senior MPs. In addition, several respondents refer to another structural problem: the need for *campaign support*. Young adults in their 20s and 30s seldom have the necessary financial and human resources to launch a successful campaign. Hence they might need funds from parties to run for office. We believe that we cannot overstate the role of campaign support in settings where money is a prerequisite for campaigning, such as the United States. Another solution would be the abolition of private funding for campaigns. For example, if campaign funding would be public and each party would get a set amount of money, imbalances in how much money a candidate could spend would be smaller. This in turn would lead to a more equal playing field because it is the parties and not the individual candidates who receive the money.

Aside from these more structural or institutional characteristics, several respondents in Sweden and even more so in Switzerland mention the need to *change the dominant political culture* in the two countries. In the words of a 23-year-old Swiss candidate:

> Youth must feel welcome, they must feel that are an integral part of their party, that their views are equally important than the ones of more senior members, and that they receive strong encouragement to run.

We believe that part of this welcoming culture is that middle-aged and senior party members should stop practices such as belittling youth, viewing them as less valuable because of their lack of political experience, and brushing aside their requests when it comes to the selection of internal or external offices. Over the past decades, parties in Sweden and Switzerland have made some advances to overcome a culture of masculinity. We believe that it is now also time that they suppress the culture of seniority, which does not perceive young adults as equally qualified representatives. In Sweden, there are sign that this is currently happening, but in Switzerland, this is less obvious.

Yet it is not only parties but also societies as a whole that should become more youth friendly. However, what concrete societies can do to open up for youth remains a difficult question. A respondent from Switzerland calls this "the million-dollar question." He illustrates that the burden is not only on parties but also on citizens, whose demand after all is an important factor. This applies particularly to Switzerland, where citizens could vote in favor of these youth lists to send more youth to parliament. However, in the majority, they refrain from doing so. Of course, this lukewarm support for youth lists could have connections to the low voter turnout of young adults. To increase youth turnout and to provide an indirect solution to the problem of youth underrepresentation, one middle-aged male respondent in Switzerland suggested increasing civic education in school. This reasoning ties again to our vicious cycle of alienation introduced in chapter 2, where the low level of participation among youth connects to their lacking interest in formal politics. As a potential remedy to these negative spirals we also advocate for increased civic education in school and university. This could then increase youths' political interest and knowledge, which in turn could increase youth turnout.

CHAPTER 8

CONCLUSIONS

> How many world leaders, for how many decades have seen and known what is coming but have decided that it is more politically expedient to keep it behind closed doors? My generation and the generations after me do not have that luxury. In the year 2050, I will be 56 years old. Yet right now, the average age of this 52nd Parliament is 49 years old.
>
> (NEW ZEALAND MP CHLÖE SWARBRICK,
> QUOTED ON CNN 2019)

As Chlöe Swarbrick, a 25-year-old member of the New Zealand Parliament, took the floor of the House during a debate in November 2019, she voiced concern of how impending global warming will affect a generation not sufficiently represented in the lawmaking assembly. When heckled by an older legislator during her address, she replied promptly "OK Boomer"—referring to the Internet meme that uses this catchphrase to mock conservative attitudes of the baby boomer generation—and continued her speech. Her talk, which intended to back a law aiming to reduce carbon emissions in New Zealand, quickly spread in the global news; the media discussed it as a sign of a rift between generations, now evident among lawmakers (CNN 2019; Washington Post 2019).

Besides the issue of climate change, where young activists have recently called for swift action, the perceived clash between the needs of younger generations and the weak response by older legislators is a feature of other debates. For instance, in 2018 youth in the United States gathered in masses—notably through the vast March for Our Lives—to protest against the inability of older politicians to regulate access to weapons that enable school shootings that primarily harm the young. Furthermore, the COVID-19 pandemic, which was still ongoing when we wrote this book, is another example of events that might affect younger and older generations heterogeneously. COVID-19 is much more dangerous and lethal for the older generations. However, the measures governments have imposed to dampen the pandemic will possibly disproportionally hit young people. As a news headline noted in early April 2020, when the pandemic-related lockdown in United States made an initial blow to the economy: "COVID-19: Young workers in the US are likely to be hit the hardest" (World Economic Forum 2020). The reason for such effects is that service-based industries, such as hospitality and retail, are more likely to have a young workforce. The Pew Research Center similarly noted that industries with a higher risk for unemployment due to COVID-19 more often employ young adults (Kochhar and Barroso 2020). In addition, COVID-19 will have some more indirect effects on younger generations. They will likely have to pay back the enormous debt that countries have been incurring in 2020 and 2021 (and probably beyond) to support the economic recovery. We therefore wish to illustrate that these unfolding events could be a potential source for even more visible conflicts between generations in society. These conflicts could potentially also play out in parliaments.

Although the tension between the interests of younger generations and those of their elders in legislatures around the globe is becoming more salient, the political world, as well as the academic literature, has not extensively discussed the problem of youths' lack of representation. In fact, one of the objections to focusing on young legislators has sometimes been the issue of "experience"—that is, it is understandable that youth are absent from higher positions since they supposedly lack the skills to shoulder such responsibilities. In the literature and larger debate, these thoughts are present as well. For instance, former speaker of the U.S. House of Representatives, James Beauchamp Clark, noted in his autobiography that "No sane man would for one moment think of making a graduate from West Point a full general, or one from Annapolis an admiral. . . . In every walk of life 'men must tarry at Jericho till their beards are grown'" (Clark 1920, 290). As we conclude this book, we want to challenge this argument head-on. While we understand the notion that some positions in the political sphere might require individuals with amassed experience, we believe that there must be some space for youth as well. This is even more relevant, considering that what we normally refer to as young people in politics are not always junior persons.

A person aged 30 or 35 years has often accumulated a rather large experience of holding lower-ranking office by this time, especially if they started their political career early on. In this sense, we also believe that there is some societal tendency to exaggerate how old someone should be to hold office. To illustrate, the United States has had presidents such as Theodore Roosevelt and John F. Kennedy who were around 43 years old when they took office, and we do not see that their age was to their detriment. More generally, we think there is merit in the argument that young people—with a different perspective and set of interests—actually bring something to the table when they enter legislatures. We also want to question the argument that age has no bearing on how an MP behaves in parliament. For instance, several respondents in Sweden and Switzerland have voiced the opinion that the age of the legislator is not important to how they think, act, or vote, and that more senior parliamentarians can be equally good representatives for younger cohorts of society as younger MPs. This observation might well be true for individual legislators, but taken together the limited evidence we present in chapter 2 points in the direction that young parliamentarians are more likely to represent the interests of younger cohorts better than more senior ones. Furthermore, the absence of youth in decision-making bodies is problematic not only substantially but also from a symbolic perspective. Young adults need representatives to whom they can relate. More likely than not, these representatives are younger MPs. Without such representatives, they are more likely to become disillusioned by conventional politics and further refrain from voting and engaging in party politics.

There are several solutions various political actors can adopt to improve youth representation and to break the vicious cycle of political alienation. Table 32 summarizes the different reforms we identify at the country level, party level, and the levels of individual MPs, candidates, and voters.[1] At the country level, the findings from our statistical models point to two institutional factors—candidate age requirements and, to a somewhat lesser extent, PR electoral systems. Both age requirements to run for office set at 18 years (or possibly even 16 years) and PR systems increase the share of youth in parliament. In particular, when it comes to candidate age requirements, we see no reason for why young adults aged 18, who have most rights and duties at this age, are not able to run for political office. Restricting young adults from running is also not compatible with the notion of becoming a citizen. At the age of 18 countries can draft youth and potentially send them to war. However, youth at this age are in several countries hindered to run for office and participate in the writing, decision-making, and implementation of legislation. Even allowing youth to vote and run for office at 16 years of age should not be a taboo topic, especially considering that in several low-income countries the median age of the population is under 20 years. Admittedly, changing the electoral system is much more difficult. Contrary

---

1. While our models do not suggest that regime type is a main predictor of the share of young MPs, becoming a democracy is the foundation for many of the reforms we envision, such as having voters freely electing their leaders.

Table 32. Suggestions on how to improve youths' political representation

Country level	Party level	MPs and candidates	Voters
Age requirement for candidacy set at 18 (or possibly 16) years	Elect young party leaders	Recognize the problem of youths' underrepresentation	Vote for young candidates
Proportional representation electoral system	Voluntary party quotas	Create an accommodating culture for youth	Show increased interests to campaigns by youth parties and young candidates
Legislative age quotas or reserved seats for young adults	Strengthen youth wings	Abolish (informal) rules inside and outside parliaments that give preferential treatment to the most senior legislators	Pressure parties to include more youth in electable districts/ positions
Term limits on political office	Support young candidates in their campaigns		Push authorities to transparently document the absence of young adults as candidates and MPs in statistics and public reports

to lowering the age of candidacy requirements, electoral systems not only affect the age of legislators but also affect the party system, the accountability between voters and legislators, and the conflict lines in society (Fiva and Folke 2016).

In addition, countries could adopt two more reforms to rectify the gross imbalance in the political representation of young adults. The first of these reforms is the implementation of youth quotas. In 2021, enforced legislative youth quotas or reserved seats are the anomaly rather than the rule in contemporary parliaments across the globe. In the few countries with such regulations, the youth quota is either too low to make a difference or not stringently implemented. Yet the experience we have with gender quotas points to the potential that youth quotas have. The increase in women's representation from single digits in the 1990s to a more respectable 25 percent in contemporary parliaments would not have been possible without the adoption of gender quotas (see Krook 2009; Kerevel 2019). What is possible for women as a group should also be possible for young adults. It seems that a crucial factor that is lacking in most countries is the political will to implement a youth quota of a respectable number, such as 20 or 25 percent, and to put in place sanctioning mechanisms to make sure these rules are enforced. For youth representation in cabinets, such quota regulations would be even more beneficial, given the infinitesimally small number of young ministers across the globe.

Another possible reform would be the implementation of limits on the time representatives can hold a certain seat or office. Several of our respondents raised this possibility. We believe that it would probably be too radical to advocate term limits of one or two terms, given that parliamentary experience and connections are important assets that MPs should possess to carry out the authority to legislate. However, setting term limits at 16 to 20 years (i.e., four terms of four or five years) seems to be a good compromise. This would allow for enough consistency for the parliament to run smoothly, but also for much needed renewal. In addition, the adoption of such term limits would be a measure that all newcomers—not only young ones—would benefit from. We do not see this proposal as unrealistic, and we hope that it might find more traction in the broader public debate in the future. Today, such rules exist for roles such as mayors, governors, or heads of state in many countries. In fact, term limits are also widespread in state legislatures in settings such as the United States (Carey et al. 2009). While not very common today (Schwindt-Bayer 2005; Council of Europe 2019), extending such principles to the national legislature for even more countries seems like a reasonable goal. We also see no reason that we could not implement the same term limits for the executive branch; that is, besides the head of the government this could also apply for ministers.

In several parliaments across the globe, the informal "principle of seniority" gives benefits to those that have served for longer periods than others. In several countries, including Sweden and the United States, the most senior members of the legislature have preferential treatment in choosing assignments and the like. In the U.S. Senate, the principle of seniority is one of the main guiding principles. According to Goodwin (1959), this principle "is more than a means of choosing committee chairmen; it is a means of assigning members to committees, of choosing subcommittee chairmen and conference committee members. It affects the deference shown to legislators on the floor, the assignment of office space, even invitations to dinners" (412). Goodwin continues, saying, "In short, it is a spirit pervading the total behavior of Congress." Over the past 60 years, very little has changed with this principle. The responses from candidates and legislators in Sweden and Switzerland lead us to believe that similar rules to the one in the United States exist in Sweden and Switzerland as well. Magni-Berton and Panel

(2021) note that the political elite in a country with an older leadership has a fundamental incentive to keep such formal and informal rules in place; it shields them from the influence of newcomers. We believe that parliaments should analyze and reform many of these principles of seniority.

Aside from these general guidelines, it is also important that countries adopt coherent and fair policies for political recruitment. We could display the Swiss electoral system as an example of country-specific institutional arrangements that function as an exclusion mechanism for young adults. The Swiss electoral system allows multiple lists by the same party. The problem with this arrangement is that, more often than not, nearly all youth face relegation to the youth list. However, these youth lists at the cantonal level rarely get enough votes to elect anybody to parliament. To rectify this subtle discrimination, we do not recommend the abolition of these youth lists, because they provide vital experience and campaign socialization for youth. Rather, we suggest legislation specifying that youth lists are only allowed if parties also place a certain percentage of candidates on the main lists.

Parties can also contribute to a rejuvenation of parliaments and cabinets. From our study, it seems that among the most efficient ways to do so is the selection of a young party leader. Parties with young party leaders also have younger parliamentary caucuses. This also holds true for cabinets with a young head of government. The second party-related factor we have identified is more subtle. Older parties also tend to select older representatives and cabinet members. Of course, we do not suggest that older parties disband, but it is important that the party elites of established parties are aware of these tendencies, which likely develop due to entrenchment of homosocial networks by powerful interests within parties. Raising this awareness could potentially entice actors with an agenda of renewal and reform in such parties to put countering measures in place, such as voluntary party quotas. Those schemes could work against the old age of the parliamentary caucuses and hopefully also within the governing boards of parties. Pertaining to party quotas, it also seems, from the example of the Swedish Social Democratic Party, that the informal goal of having 25 per cent of the seats on lists allotted to young adults works well. Implicitly, this decision might have also persuaded other parties in Sweden to balance their lists, as representatives from these parties also state that they try to conform to the age in society when nominating their lists. A further relevant feature of parties is active and strong youth wings. The survey of Swedish MPs and candidates highlights that strong youth wings can be a force in nominating younger aspiring politicians. Finding ways to strengthen youth wings—for instance, by giving them real power in the party, including influence in nominations for elected office—could be something to which parties in other countries could aspire to as well. It would also demonstrate to youth that they have a place within the party, including in decision-making processes. Beyond these more formal arrangements, party leaders and elites could remind themselves that intergenerational justice can only be achieved if youth gain greater access to positions of power—be it in the party leadership, elected office, or even in the executive.

Youths' underrepresentation is also a question of awareness for candidates and MPs. Our insights from the Swiss example suggest that many politicians are reluctant to confront the problem of young adults' lack of representation. They give contradictory answers when asked whether youths' lack of parliamentary presence is a problem. On the one hand, a majority of respondents affirm that they would prefer the parliament to reflect the Swiss population in terms of its age distribution, something that should clearly imply an increase in young MPs. On the other hand, many of the same respondents answer that there is no systematic discrimination against youth in nominations and elections. This implies that they turn a blind eye on one of the problems in contemporary representative democracies, even if we cannot judge here whether or not they do so deliberately. Similarly, Swiss survey respondents mentioned that they would welcome more young adults on lists, but they still referred to a lack of youth willing to run on main lists and even noted that young adults complain rather than engaging in becoming an active part of politics. To us, respondents might offer these answers out of expediency rather than conviction. More broadly, this reluctance among elite actors to acknowledge youth underrepresentation is linked to the problem of a larger political culture that is still not welcoming to young adults. Attitudes suggesting that youth are not "experienced" enough ignore the vital forces of rejuvenation to politics that young adults might bring. These examples further illustrate this political culture that is still rather unfriendly to youth. It is also important to note that the gains youth have made in a few countries are not without resistance. In Sweden, for example, youths' increased representation faces some opposition from more senior politicians. Yet, even more importantly, there are instances where youth face condescending and belittling attitudes from senior legislators. These views risk isolating young newcomers and we think this problem requires further attention in politics and in society at large.

If we care about young adults' concerns, ideas, and proposals, this political culture of seniority within parliaments, parties, and political elites must change, not only in Switzerland and Sweden but also throughout the world. Prominent examples of women's activism inside and outside parliament that have advanced gender equality, for instance through the #MeToo movement, illustrate that activism can end discrimination—or at least alleviate it. Similar activism could also improve the standing of young adults. An example is the "Not Too Young to Run" movement, a global campaign that promotes and supports young people's participation in politics. Stemming from Nigeria in 2016, this campaign has gained traction in international bodies (see United Nations 2016b), and we see it as a promising attempt to bring attention to youth underrepresentation. It is a rallying cry geared toward abolishing barriers that hinder young adults' chances to stand for office. Examples of the work of this campaign come from Gambia, where young adults without a party affiliation received support to stand for office, something that they would not have done otherwise (see Women Deliver 2017). Moreover, in recent years, youth have awakened to and led climate and antigun activism. If youth show sustained engagement in the years to come, they might break the conventional barriers young adults face in politics, albeit slowly.

Finally, we want to point to the role that ordinary citizens can take to support young adults in their struggle to gain a larger share in decision-making. In countries where there is a large pool of candidates, such as Switzerland, this can be as simple as casting a vote for a young politician. In other countries, making a deliberate choice for young candidates might be harder because there might not be any youth for whom to vote. In a first-past-the-post system, voters can only vote for a young candidate if one of the two (or three or four) candidates is young. In closed-list proportional representation systems, voters must accept the predetermined order of candidates. If no young candidate is on their preferred list, they cannot do much. However, what citizens can do, regardless of the context, is to lobby for youth, because parties might listen once there is enough demand. Unfortunately, the pressure to include young adults is low in most countries. Yet the Swedish example shows that the political culture can change, even if not everyone agrees on making the Riksdag younger.

Quo vadis, youth representation? Despite the fact that we have shown in many avenues how youth representation can improve, we do not think that, in the short run, we will have major improvements to youths' representation in parliaments and cabinets. While there are positive signs of increased youth engagement in areas such as climate change or gun control, as well as some youth activism for democracy in more authoritarian countries, the vicious cycle of youth alienation seems to remain a reality for many young adults across the globe. It will be very hard to break this cycle, not least because many stakeholders, including parties, governments, and (older) voters, seem to be content with the political disengagement of youth. Youth underrepresentation in parliaments and cabinets is also an institutionalized feature in many settings. Over the past 30 or 40 years, very little has changed in youth representation, at least if we generalize from the four countries we have analyzed in detail (i.e., Australia, France, Germany and the United Kingdom). Judging by the current low share of young MPs in other countries as well, there could hardly have been any increase in these countries over the past decades either.

We also see tendencies of acquiescence with the issue of youths' absence in politics within academia and the scholarly literature. Compared to work on the political marginalization of other social groups, such as women or ethnic minorities, research on young adults has been scarce. We hope that with this book we have shed some light on how few youth are actually in positions of political power. In particular, the age group of people aged 35 years or under faces rampant underrepresentation: they make up about 10 percent of all parliamentarians and a mere 3 percent of ministers across the globe in 2019. This means that young adults face levels of underrepresentation at a ratio of more than one to three in parliament and one to ten in cabinet, when compared to the voting-age population. For the age group of MPs aged 40 years or under, the underrepresentation is a bit less pronounced but still in the vicinity of one to two for parliamentarians and one to five for cabinet members. Moreover, we must remind ourselves that these numbers are conservative, since we have measured the age of politicians at the beginning of each term. By the end of these terms, the age gap is even larger. Furthermore, in the calculation of these ratios between the age of politicians and citizens, we have also excluded those under 18 years. If we were to calculate youths' underrepresentation of the whole population, looking also at children and adolescents, the gap between youths' political representation and their share in the citizenry would widen dramatically. We do not necessarily advocate such calculations, because we find the assumption of focusing on a limit of adulthood set at 18 years old to be a reasonable benchmark. However, what we strongly propose in this book is that young adults deserve an increased presence in legislatures, cabinets, and in other political posts as well. While it will be hard to change course, we hope that we have at least raised some awareness of this pressing generational injustice.

References

Abbink, J. (2005). "Being Young in Africa: The Politics of Despair and Renewal." In J. Abbink and I. van Kessel (eds.), *Vanguards or Vandals: Youth, Politics and Conflict in Africa*, 1–33. Leiden: Brill.

Abramson, P., and R. F. Inglehart (2009). *Value change in global perspective*. Ann Arbor: University of Michigan Press.

Achen, C., and T. Y. Wang (2019). "Declining voter turnout in Taiwan: A generational effect?" *Electoral Studies* 58: 113–24.

Acuña-Duarte, A. A. (2017). "Electoral apathy among Chilean youth: New evidence for the voter registration dilemma." *Estudios Gerenciales* 33 (145): 341–51.

Alesina, A., T. Cassidy, and U. Troiano (2019). "Old and young politicians." *Economica* 86: 689–727.

Ansolabehere, S., and J. M. Snyder Jr. (2002). "The incumbency advantage in US elections: An analysis of state and federal offices, 1942–2000." *Election Law journal* 1 (3): 315–38.

Bailer, S., C. Breunig, N. Giger, and A. M. Wust (2022). "The Diminishing Value of Representing the Disadvantaged: Between Group Representation and Individual Career Paths." *British Journal of Political Science* 52 (2): 535–52.

Bale, T., P. Webb, and M. Poletti. (2019). *Footsoldiers: Political party membership in the 21st Century*. London: Routledge.

Bannon, D. (2004). "Marketing segmentation and political marketing." Paper presented to the UK Political Studies Association conference, University of Lincoln.

Barrett, M., and D. Pachi (eds.) (2019). *Youth civic and political engagement*. London: Routledge.

Bauer, G., and M. Tremblay (eds.) (2011). *Women and Executive Power*. London: Routledge.

BBC (2018). "Emile Ratelband, 69, told he cannot legally change his age" December 3. https://www.bbc.com/news/world-europe-46425774

Beauregard, K. (2014). "Gender, political participation and electoral systems: A cross-national analysis." *European Journal of Political Research* 53 (3): 617–34.

Bego, I. (2013). "Accessing power in new democracies: The Appointment of Female Ministers in Postcommunist Europe." *Political Research Quarterly* 67 (2): 347–60.

Belschner, J. (2021) "The adoption of youth quotas after the Arab uprisings." *Politics, Groups, and Identities* 9 (1): 151–69.

Belschner, J., and M. Garcia de Paredes (2020). "Hierarchies of Representation: The Re-distributive Effects of Gender and Youth Quotas." *Representation* 57 (1): 1–20.

Ben-Bassat, A., and M. Dahan (2012). "Social identity and voting behavior." *Public Choice* 151 (1–2): 193–214.

Berger, A. A. (2017). *Political parties: A sociological study of the oligarchical tendencies of modern democracy*. New York: Routledge.

Bergh, J. (eds.) (2014). *"Stemmerett for 16-åringer Resultater fra evalueringen av forsøket med senket stemmerettsalder ved lokalvalget 2011."* Institutt for samfunnsforskning, Rapport 1. https://www.regjeringen.no/globalassets/upload/kmd/ko mm/rapporter/rapport_stemmerett_for_16-aaringer.pdf

Berry, C. (2008). "Labour's Lost Youth: Young People and the Labour Party's Youth Sections." *The Political Quarterly* 79: 366–76.

Bhatti, Y., and K. Hansen (2012). "The effect of generation and age on turnout to the European Parliament—How turnout will continue to decline in the future." *Electoral Studies* 31 (2): 262–72.

Bhatti, Y., K. Hansen, and H. Wass (2012). "The relationship between age and turnout: A roller-coaster ride." *Electoral Studies* 31 (3): 588–93.

Bidadanure, J. (2015a). "Better Procedures for Fairer Outcomes: Can Youth Quotas Increase Our Chances of Meeting the Demands of Intergenerational Justice?" In J. Tremmel, A. Mason, P. Haakenstad, and G. I. Dimitrijoski (eds.), *Youth Quotas and Other Efficient Forms of Youth Participation in Ageing Societies*, 37–55. The Netherlands: Springer Verlaag.

Bidadanure, J. (2015b). "Better Procedures for Fairer Outcomes: Youth Quotas in Parliaments." *Intergenerational Justice Review* 1 (1): 1–7.

Bidadanure, J. U. (2021). *Justice across ages: Treating young and old as equals*. Oxford: Oxford University Press.

Binstock, R. H. (2012). "Older Voters and the 2010 U.S. Election: Implications for 2012 and Beyond?" *Gerontologist* 52 (3): 408–17.

Bjarnegård, E. (2013). *Gender, Informal Institutions and Political Recruitment: Explaining Male Dominance in Parliamentary Representation*. London: Palgrave Macmillan.

Bjarnegård, E. (2018). "Focusing on Masculinity and Male-Dominated Networks in Corruption." In H. Stensöta and L. Wängnerud (eds.), *Gender and Corruption: Historical Roots and New Avenues for Research*, 257–73. Cham: Springer International Publishing.

Bjarnegård, E., and M. Kenny (2015). "Revealing the 'secret garden': The informal dimensions of political recruitment." *Politics & Gender* 11 (4): 748–53.

Blais, A. (2000). *To vote or not to vote: The merits and limits of rational choice theory*. Pittsburgh: University of Pittsburgh Press.

Blais, A. (2014). "Why is turnout so low in Switzerland? Comparing the attitudes of Swiss and German citizens towards electoral democracy." *Swiss Political Science Review* 20 (4): 520–28.

Blais, A., E. Gidengil, N. Nevitte, and R. Nadeau (2004). "Where Does Turnout Decline Come From?" *European Journal of Political Research* 43: 221–36.

Blais, A., and P. Loewen (2011). *Youth electoral engagement in Canada*. Ottawa: Elections Canada.

Blaydes, L., and D. A. Linzer (2008). "The Political Economy of Women's Support for Fundamentalist Islam." *World Politics* 60 (4): 576–609.

Blondel, J. (2014). *Comparative Government Introduction*. London: Routledge.

Bob-Milliar, G. M. (2014) "Party Youth Activists and Low-Intensity Electoral Violence in Ghana: A Qualitative Study of Party Foot Soldiers' Activism." *African Studies Quarterly* 15 (1): 125–52.

Bogaards, M. (2013). "The choice for proportional representation: Electoral system design in peace agreements." *Civil Wars* 15(1) : 71–87.

Borelli, M. (2010). "Gender Desegregation and Gender Integration in the President's Cabinet, 1933–2010." *Presidential Studies Quarterly* 40 (4): 734–49.

Bouie, J. (2018). "Let the teens vote: States would do well to extend the Franchise to 16-year-olds." *Slate.* https://slate.com/news-and-politics/2018/04/states-would-do-well-to-enfranchise-16-year-olds.html

Briggs, J. (2017). *Young People and Political Participation: Teen Players.* New York: Palgrave Macmillan.

Brooks, R., K. Byford, and K. Sela (2015). "The changing role of students' unions within contemporary higher education." *Journal of Education Policy* 30 (2): 165–81.

Bruni, F. (2019). "In defense of the gerontocracy." *New York Times*, February 27. https://www.nytimes.com/2019/02/26/opinion/older-politicians.html

Bruter, M., and S. Harrison (2009). *The future of our democracies? Young party members in six European democracies.* New York: Palgrave Macmillan.

Bryan, S. (2010). "The Youth Bulge in Africa: Opportunities for Constructive Engagement in the Political Process." National Democratic Institute. https://www.ndi.org/sites/default/files/Youth_Bulge_Africa_102710.pdf

Bunis, D. (2018). "The Immense Power of the Older Voter." *AAARP Bulletin.* https://www.aarp.org/politics-society/government-elections/info-2018/power-role-older-voters.html

Cancela, J., A. Dias, and M. Lisi (2017). "The impact of endorsements in intra-party elections: Evidence from open primaries in a new Portuguese party." *Politics* 37 (2): 167–83.

Carey, J. M. (1998). *Term Limits and Legislative Representation.* New York: Cambridge University Press.

Carey, J. M., R. G. Niemi, and L. W. Powell (2009). *Term limits in state legislatures.* Ann Arbor: University of Michigan Press.

Caul, M. (2001). "Political parties and the adoption of candidate gender quotas: A cross–national analysis." *Journal of Politics* 63 (4): 1214–29.

CCS. (2019). Comparative Candidates Survey Module II—2013–2018 [Dataset—cumulative file]. Distributed by FORS, Lausanne.

Celis, K., and S. Childs (2008). "The Descriptive and Substantive Representation of Women: New Directions." *Parliamentary Affairs* 61 (3): 419–25.

Central Intelligence Agency (2019a). "Country Comparison: Median Age." *The World Factbook.* https://www.cia.gov/library/publications/the-world-factbook/fields/343rank.html

Central Intelligence Agency (2019b). "Religions." *The World Factbook.* https://www.cia.gov/library/publications/the-world-factbook/fields/print_2122.html

Childs, S., and P. Webb (2012). *Sex, gender and the Conservative Party: From iron lady to kitten heels.* London: Palgrave Macmillan.

Childs, S. L., and M. C. Kittilson (2016). "Feminizing political parties: Women's party member organizations within European parliamentary parties." *Party Politics* 22 (5): 598–608.

Clark, C. (1920). *My Quarter Century in American Politics*. New York: Harper and Brothers.

Claveria, S. (2014). "Still a 'Male business'? Explaining women's presence in executive office." *West European Politics* 37 (5): 1156–76.

CNN (2019). "A 25-year-old politician got heckled during a climate crisis speech. Her deadpan retort: 'OK, boomer.'" https://edition.cnn.com/2019/11/06/asia/new-zeal and-ok-boomer-trnd/index.html

Coleman, S. (2017). "How democracies have disengaged from young people." In B. D. Loader (ed.), *Young Citizens in the Digital Age: Political Engagement, Young People and New Media*, 166–85. London: Routledge.

Conover, P. J. (1988). "The Role of Social Groups in Political Thinking." *British Journal of Political Science* 18 (1): 51–76.

Cordero, G., and X. Coller (eds.) (2018). *Democratizing Candidate Selection: New Methods, Old Receipts?* New York: Palgrave Macmillan.

Council of Europe (2019). Report on term limits, by the Venice Commission. Opinion No. 908/2017. https://www.venice.coe.int/webforms/documents/default.aspx?pdf file=CDL-AD(2019)007-e

Cox, G. W., and J. N. Katz (1996). "Why did the incumbency advantage in US House elections grow?" *American Journal of Political Science* 40 (2): 478–97.

Cross, W., and L. Young (2004). "The Contours of Political Party Membership in Canada." *Party Politics* 10: 427–44.

Cross, W., and L. Young (2008). "Factors influencing the decision of the young politically engaged to join a political party: An investigation of the Canadian case." *Party Politics* 14 (3): 345–69.

Crowder-Meyer, M. (2013). "Gendered recruitment without trying: How local party recruiters affect women's representation." *Politics & Gender* 9 (4): 390–413.

Curry, J. M., and M. R. Haydon (2018). "Lawmaker age, issue salience, and senior representation in congress." *American Politics Research* 46 (4): 567–95.

Curtin, J. (2014). "Conservative women and executive office in Australia and New Zealand." In K. Celis and S. Childs (eds.), *Gender, Conservatism and Political Representation*. Colchester: ECPR Press.

Dahlerup, D. (2007). "Electoral gender quotas: Between equality of opportunity and equality of result." *Representation* 43 (2): 73–92.

Dahlerup, D., and M. Leyenaar (eds.) (2013). *Breaking male dominance in old democracies*. Oxford: Oxford University Press.

Dahlum, S., and T. Wig (2021). "Chaos on Campus: Universities and Mass Political Protest." *Comparative Political Studies* 54 (1): 3–32.

Dalton, R. J. (2008). *The good citizen: How a younger generation is reshaping American politics*. Washington, DC: CQ Press.

Davidson, S., and R. H. Binstock (2011). "Political marketing and segmentation in aging democracies." In J. Lees-Marshment (ed.), *Routledge Handbook of Political Marketing*, 20–33. London: Routledge.

Delli Carpini, M. X. (2000). "Gen.com: Youth, civic engagement, and the new information environment." *Political Communication* 17 (4): 341–49.

Delli Carpini, M. X., and S. Keeter (1996). *What Americans know about politics and why it matters*. New Haven: Yale University Press.

Dermody, J., S. Hanmer-Lloyd, and R. Scullion (2010). "Young people and voting behaviour: Alienated youth and (or) an interested and critical citizenry?" *European Journal of Marketing* 44 (3–4): 421–35.

De Roon, C. (2020). "Party youth wing membership in the Netherlands: The role of organization-level characteristics." *Acta Politica* 55 (4): 629–47.

Dobbs, K. L. (2020). "Youth quotas and 'Jurassic Park' politicians: Age as a heuristic for vote choice in Tunisia's new democracy." *Democratization* 27: 990–1005.

Dostie-Goulet, E. (2009). "Social networks and the development of political interest." *Journal of Youth Studies* 12 (4): 405–21.

Douglas, J. (2020). "Lowering the Voting Age from the Ground up: The United States' Experience in Allowing 16-Year Olds to Vote." In J. Eichhorn and J. Bergh (eds.), *Lowering the Voting Age to 16: Learning from Real Experiences Worldwide*. Basingstoke: Palgrave Macmillan.

Eichhorn, J., and J. Bergh (eds.) (2020). *Lowering the Voting Age to 16*. Basingstoke: Palgrave Macmillan.

Erikson, J., and C. Josefsson (2021). "Equal playing field? On the intersection between gender and being young in the Swedish Parliament." *Politics, Groups, and Identities* 9 (1): 81–100.

Erlingsson, G. O., and R. Öhrvall (2010). *Politikens villkor: Om engagemang och avhopp i kommunpolitiken*. Linköping: Centrum för kommunstrategiska studier.

Eshima, S., and D. M. Smith (2022). "Just a Number? Voter Evaluations of Age in Candidate Choice Experiments." *The Journal of Politics*, forthcoming.

Escobar-Lemmon, M., and M. M. Taylor-Robinson (2005). "Women ministers in Latin American government: When, where, and why." *American Journal of Political Science* 49 (4): 829–44.

ESS (2016). "European Social Survey Round 8: Data file edition 2.1." NSD—Norwegian Centre for Research Data, Norway—Data Archive and distributor of ESS data for ESS ERIC.

EveryPolitican (2019). The world's richest open dataset on politicians. https://everypolitician.org/

Faas, D. (2007). "Youth, Europe and the nation: The political knowledge, interests and identities of the new generation of European youth." *Journal of Youth Studies* 10 (2): 161–81.

Favero, A. (2019). "Surprises in Switzerland's Election: A Green Surge, More Women, and Decline for Populist SVP." https://eaworldview.com/2019/10/the-surprises-in-switzerland-election-green-surge-more-women-decline-populist-svp/

Fawcett, M. (2018). *Women's Suffrage*. Moscow: Litres.

Fiva, J. H., and O. Folke (2016). "Mechanical and psychological effects of electoral reform." *British Journal of Political Science* 46 (2): 265–79.

Flanagan, C. (2016). "Epilogue: Youth and the 'Social Contract.'" In P. Thijssen, J. Siongers, J. Van Laer, J. Haers, and S. Mels (eds.), *Political Engagement of the Young in Europe: Youth in the Crucible*, 195–203. London: Routledge.

Franceschet, S., and J. M. Piscopo (2014). "Sustaining gendered practices? Power, parties, and elite political networks in Argentina." *Comparative Political Studies* 47 (1): 85–110.

Franklin, M. (2004). *Voter turnout and the dynamics of electoral competition in established democracies since 1945.* New York: Cambridge University Press.

Fredriksson, P. G., and L. Wang (2011). "Sex and environmental policy in the U.S. house of representatives." *Economics Letters* 113 (3): 228–30.

Freechild Institute for Youth Engaement (2019). "Youth in Politics." https://freechild .org/youth-and-politics/

Furlong, A., and F. Cartmel (2012). "Social Change and Political Engagement among Young People: Generation and the 2009/2010 British Election Survey." *Parliamentary Affairs* 65 (1): 13–28.

Gallagher, M., and M. Marsh (2004). "Party Membership in Ireland: The Members of Fine Gael." *Party Politics* 10: 407–26.

Gallup (2018). "Global Warming Age Gap: Younger Americans Most Worried." https://news.gallup.com/poll/234314/global-warming-age-gap-younger-america ns-worried.aspx

Giger, N., and J. Bernauer (2009). "Electoral Institutions, Party Positioning and Individual Policy Congruence. A Multilevel Analysis of Parliamentary Democracies." Unpublished manuscript.

Given, C. (2018). "Sorry, 'March for Our Lives' kids, that's not how politics works." *Washington Examiner*, March 28. https://www.washingtonexaminer.com/opinion /sorry-march-for-our-lives-kids-thats-not-how-politics-works

Goddard, D. (2019). "Entering the men's domain? Gender and portfolio allocation in European governments." *European Journal of Political Research* 58 (2): 631–55.

Goerres, A. (2007). "Why are Older People More Likely to Vote? The Impact of Ageing on Electoral Turnout in Europe." *British Journal of Politics and International Relations* 9 (1): 90–121.

Golosov, G. V. (2014). "Growing Old without Grace: Electoral Authoritarianism and the Age Composition of Russia's Regional Legislative Assemblies." *Representation* 50 (4): 509–26.

Goodwin, G. (1959). "The Seniority System in Congress." *American Political Science Review* 53 (2): 412–36.

Government of Norway (2011). "Fleire unge politikarar der unge røyster" [More young politicians where youth are voting]. Kommunal-og regionaldepartementet. https://www.regjeringen.no/no/dokumentarkiv/stoltenberg-ii/krd/Nyheter-og-pr essemeldinger/pressemeldinger/2011/fleire-unge-politikarar-der-unge-royster/id 667415/

Grasso, M. T. (2014) "Age, Period and Cohort Analysis in a Comparative Context: Political Generations and Political Participation Repertoires in Western Europe." *Electoral Studies* 33: 63–76.

Hainz, T. (2015). "Are Youth Quotas a Form of Ageism?" In J. Tremmel, A. Mason, P. Haakenstad, and G. I. Dimitrijoski (eds.), *Youth quotas and other efficient forms of youth participation in ageing societies*, 21–35. Berlin: Springer Verlaag.

Hajek, L. (2019). "Effects of age and tenure on MPs' legislative behaviour in the Czech Republic." *Journal of Legislative Studies* 25 (4): 553–75.

Hamlin, J. K., N. Mahajan, Z. Liberman, and K. Wynn (2013). "Not like me = bad: Infants prefer those who harm dissimilar others." *Psychological Science* 24 (4): 589–94.

Hannan-Morrow, S., and M. Roden (2014). "Gender, Age and Generational Effects on Turnout in Australian Federal Elections." Presented at Australian Political Studies Association 2014 Conference—Sydney. https://www.aec.gov.au/About_AEC/rese arch/files/apsa-2014-gender-age-and-generational-effects-on-turnout-in-australi an-federal-elections.pdf

Hansen, E. R., and S. A. Treul (2015). "The symbolic and substantive representation of LGB Americans in the US House." *Journal of Politics* 77 (4): 955–67.

Hassell, H. J. (2016). "Party control of party primaries: Party influence in nominations for the US senate." *Journal of Politics* 78 (1): 75–87.

Heclo, H. (1988). "Generational Politics." In J. L. Palmer, T. Smeeding, and B. B. Torrey (eds.), *The Vulnerable*, 381–411. Washington, DC: Urban Institute Press.

Heidar, K. (2006). "Party membership and participation." In R. S. Katz and W. J. Crotty (eds.), *Handbook of Party Politics*, 301–15. London: SAGE Publishing.

Henig, R., and S. Henig (2001). *Women and political power: Europe since 1945*. London: Routledge.

Henn, M., M. Weinstein, and D. Wring (2002). "A Generation Apart? Youth and Political Participation in Britain." *British Journal of Politics and International Relations* 4 (2): 167–92.

Henn, M., and N. Foard (2012). "Young people, political participation and trust in Britain." *Parliamentary Affairs* 65 (1): 47–67.

Hennel, L. (2010). "S missar mål om unga." *Svenska Dagbladet*, April 29. https://www .svd.se/s-missar-mal-om-unga

Holbein, J. B., and D. S. Hillygus (2016). "Making Young Voters: The Impact of Preregistration on Youth Turnout." *American Journal of Political Science* 60 (2): 364–82.

Holbein, J. B., and D. S. Hillygus (2020). *Making Young Voters: Converting Civic Attitudes into Civic Action*. New York: Cambridge University Press.

Holman, M. R., and M. C. Schneider (2018). "Gender, race, and political ambition: How intersectionality and frames influence interest in political office." *Politics, Groups, and Identities* 6 (2): 264–80.

Hooghe, M., D. Stolle, and P. Stouthuysen (2004). "Head Start in Politics: The Recruitment Function of Youth Organizations of Political Parties in Belgium (Flanders)." *Party Politics* 10 (2): 193–212.

Hooghe, M., and K. Deschouwer (2011). "Veto players and electoral reform in Belgium." *West European Politics* 34 (3): 626–43.

Hoskins, B., M. Saisana, and C. M. Villalba (2015). "Civic competence of youth in Europe: Measuring cross national variation through the creation of a composite indicator." *Social Indicators Research* 123 (2): 431–57.

Howe, P. (2010). *Citizens Adrift: The Democratic Disengagement of Young Canadians*. Vancouver: University of British Columbia Press.

Hughes, M. M. (2016). "Electoral systems and the legislative representation of Muslim ethnic minority women in the West, 2000–2010." *Parliamentary Affairs* 69 (3): 548–68.

Inglehart, I., and P. Norris (2003). *Rising tide: Gender equality and cultural change around the world*. Cambridge: Cambridge University Press.

Inter-Parliamentary Union (IPU) (2014). *Youth participation in national parliaments*. Geneva: IPU.

Inter-Parliamentary Union (IPU) (2016). *Youth participation in national parliaments*. Geneva: IPU.

Inter-Parliamentary Union (IPU) (2018). *Youth participation in national parliaments*. Geneva: IPU.

Inter-Parliamentary Union (IPU) (2019). New Parline: The IPU's Open Data Platform (beta): Your one-stop-shop for information about national parliaments. https://data.ipu.org/

Inter-Parliamentary Union (IPU) (2021). *Youth participation in national parliaments*. Geneva: IPU.

Jalalzai, F. (2013). *Shattered, cracked, or firmly intact? Women and the executive glass ceiling worldwide*. New York: Oxford University Press.

Janmaat, J. G., and A. Keating (2019). "Are today's youth more tolerant? Trends in tolerance among young people in Britain." *Ethnicities* 19 (1): 44–65.

Jennings, M. K., and L. Stoker (2004). "Social trust and civic engagement across time and generations." *Acta politica* 39 (4): 342–79.

Jennings, M. K., and R. Niemi (2014). *Generations and politics: A panel study of young adults and their parents*. Princeton: Princeton University Press.

Jiménez-Sánchez, M., X. Coller, and M. Portillo-Pérez (2018). "MPs of Traditional Parties' Perceptions on Candidate Selection in Times of Political Crisis and Reform." In G. Cordero and X. Coller (eds.), *Democratizing candidate selection: New methods, old receipts?* New York: Palgrave Macmillan.

Joshi, D. K. (2013). "The representation of younger age cohorts in Asian parliaments: Do electoral systems make a difference?" *Representation* 49 (1): 1–16.

Joshi, D. K. (2015). "The inclusion of excluded majorities in South Asian parliaments: Women, youth, and the working class." *Journal of Asian and African Studies* 50 (2): 223–38.

Joshi, D. K., and M. Och (2021). "Early birds, short tenures, and the double squeeze: How gender and age intersect with parliamentary representation." *Politics, Groups, and Identities* 9 (3): 629–45.

Kakepaki, M., F. Kountouri, L., Verzichelli, and X. Coller (2018). "The Sociopolitical Profile of Parliamentary Representatives in Greece, Italy and Spain Before and After the 'Eurocrisis': A Comparative Empirical Assessment." In G. Cordero and X. Coller (eds.), *Democratizing candidate selection: New methods, old receipts?* New York: Palgrave Macmillan.

Kaloianov, R. (2015). "What Do Quotas Do? Reflections on the Ubiquity and Justice of Quotas." In J. Tremmel, A. Mason, P. Haakenstad, and G. I. Dimitrijoski (eds.), *Youth quotas and other efficient forms of youth participation in ageing societies*, 7–19. Berlin: Springer Verlaag.

Kamikubo, M. (2019). "Age of eligibility to run for election in Japan: A barrier to political careers?" *Journal of Contemporary East Asia Studies* 8 (1): 14–29.

Karlsson, D., and M. Gilljam (eds.) (2014). *Svenska politiker. Om de folkvalda i riksdag, landsting och kommuner*. Stockholm: Santérus förlag.

Karnein, A., and D. Roser (2015) "Saving the Planet by Empowering the Young?" In J. Tremmel, A. Mason, P. Haakenstad, and G. I. Dimitrijoski (eds.), *Youth quotas and other efficient forms of youth participation in ageing societies*, 77–92. Berlin: Springer Verlaag.

Kedar, O., L. Harsgor, and R. A. Sheinerman (2016). "Are voters equal under proportional representation?" *American Journal of Political Science* 60 (3): 676–91.

Kerevel, Y. (2019). "Empowering women? Gender quotas and women's political careers." *Journal of Politics* 81 (4): 1167–80.

Kim, S.-E., and J. Urpelainen (2017). "The Polarization of American Environmental Policy: A Regression Discontinuity Analysis of Senate and House Votes, 1971–2013." *Review of Policy Research* 34 (4): 456–84.

King, R. L. (2015). "Justin Trudeau got help from youth, new voters, social media in election win." *The Star*, October 23. https://www.thestar.com/news/canada/2015/10/23/justin-trudeau-got-help-from-youth-new-voters-social-media-in-election-win.html

Kissau, K., G. Lutz, and J. Rosset (2012). "Unequal representation of age groups in Switzerland." *Representation* 48 (1): 63–81.

Kittilson, M. C. (2006). *Challenging Parties, Changing Parliaments: Women and Elected Office in Contemporary Western Europe*. Columbus: Ohio State University Press.

Kochhar, R., and A. Barroso (2020). "Young workers likely to be hard hit as COVID-19 strikes a blow to restaurants and other service sector jobs." Pew Research, March 27.https://www.pewresearch.org/fact-tank/2020/03/27/young-workers-likely-to-be-hard-hit-as-covid-19-strikes-a-blow-to-restaurants-and-other-service-sector-jobs/

Kohler, A., and A. Tognina (2019). "Record number of women running for parliament." https://www.swissinfo.ch/eng/parliamentary-elections_record-number-of-women-running-for-parliament/45217174

Kölln, A. K. (2017). "Has party members' representativeness changed over time?" In U. Andersson, J. Ohlsson, H. Oscarsson, and M. Oskarson (eds.), *Larmar och gör sig till*. Göteborg: SOM-undersökningen.

Krook, M. L. (2007). "Candidate Gender Quotas: A Framework for Analysis." *European Journal of Political Research* 46 (3): 367–94.

Krook, M. L. (2009). "Beyond supply and demand: A feminist-institutionalist theory of candidate selection." *Political Research Quarterly* 63 (4): 707–20.

Krook, M. L. (2010). *Quotas for Women in Politics: Gender and Candidate Selection Reform Worldwide*. Oxford: Oxford University Press.

Krook, M. L., and D. O'Brien (2012). "All the President's Men. The Appointment of Female Ministers Worldwide." *Journal of Politics* 74 (3): 840–55.

Krook, M. L., and M. K. Nugent (2018). "Not Too Young to Run? Age requirements and young people in elected office." *Intergenerational Justice Review* 4 (2): 60–67.

Kymlicka, W. (1995). *Multicultural Citizenship*. Oxford: Oxford University Press.

LaGraffe, D. (2012). "The youth bulge in Egypt: An intersection of demographics, security, and the Arab Spring." *Journal of Strategic Security* 5 (2): 65–80.

Larsen, M., and P. J. Pedersen (2017). "Labour force activity after 65: What explain recent trends in Denmark, Germany and Sweden?" *Journal for Labour Market Research* 50 (1): 15–27.

Lawless, J. L., and R. L. Fox (2015). *Running from office: Why young Americans are turned off to politics.* New York: Oxford University Press.

Lilleker, D. (2005). "Political marketing: The cause of the democratic deficit?" In W. W. Wymer and J. Lees-Marshment (eds.), *Current Issues in Political Marketing,* 5–26. New York: Haworth Press.

Lin, J. Y. (2012). "Youth Bulge: A Demographic Dividend or a Demographic Bomb in Developing Countries?" The World Bank (blog).https://blogs.worldbank.org/dev elopmenttalk/youth-bulge-a-demographic-dividend-or-a-demographic-bomb-in -developing-countries

Loader, B. D. (ed.) (2007). *Young citizens in the digital age: Polititical engagement, young people and new media.* London: Routledge.

Long, J. S., and J. Freese (2005). *Regression models for categorical outcomes using Stata.* College Station, PA: Stata Press.

Lupia, A., and T. S. Philpot (2005). "Views from Inside the Net: How websites affect young adults' political interest." *Journal of Politics* 67: 1122–42.

Luskin, R. C. (1990). "Explaining Political Sophistication." *Political Behavior* 12 (2): 331–61.

Magni-Berton, R., and S. Panel (2021). "Gerontocracy in a comparative perspective: Explaining why political leaders are (almost always) older than their constituents." *Sociology Compass* 15 (1): e12841.

Mansbridge, J. (1999). "Should Blacks Represent Blacks and Women Represent Women? A Contingent 'Yes.'" *Journal of Politics* 61 (3): 628–57.

Mansbridge, J. (2015). "Should workers represent workers?" *Swiss Political Science Review* 21: 261–70.

Marsh, D., T. O'Toole, and S. Jones (2007). *Young People and Politics in the UK: Apathy or Alienation?* Basingstoke: Palgrave Macmillan.

Marshall, M. G., K. Jaggers, and T. Gurr (2011). *Polity IV Project: Dataset Users' Manual.* Arlington: Polity IV Project.

Martin, A. (2012a). "Political participation among the young in Australia: Testing Dalton's good citizen thesis." *Australian Journal of Political Science* 47 (2): 211–26.

Martin, A. (2012b). *Young people and politics: Political engagement in the Anglo-American democracies.* London: Routledge.

Matland, R. E. (2005). "Enhancing women's political participation: Legislative recruitment and electoral systems." In J. Ballington and A. Karam (eds.), *Women in parliament: Beyond numbers,* 93–111. Stockholm: IDEA.

Matland, R. E., and D. T. Studlar (1996). "The contagion of women candidates in single-member district and proportional representation electoral systems: Canada and Norway." *Journal of Politics* 58 (3): 707–33.

Matthews, H., L. Melanie, and M. Taylor (1999). "Young people's participation and representation in society." *Geoforum* 30: 135–44.

McClean, C. (2019). "Does It Matter That Politicians Are Older Than Their Constituents? Yes" Paper in progress. University of California, San Diego.

McDonald, S. (2011). "What's in the 'Old Boys' Network? Accessing Social Capital in Gendered and Racialized Networks." *Social Networks* 33 (4): 317–30.

McEvoy, C. (2016). "Does the Descriptive Representation of Women Matter? A

Comparison of Gendered Differences in Political Attitudes between Voters and Representatives in the European Parliament." *Politics & Gender* 12 (4): 754–80.

McGinley, B., and A. Grieve (2010). "Maintaining the status quo? Appraising the effectiveness of youth councils in Scotland." In B. Percy-Smith and N. Thomas (eds.), *A handbook of children and young people's participation: Perspectives from theory and practice*, 254–61. London: Routledge.

McKee, P., and C. E. Barber (2001). "Plato's Theory of Aging." *Journal of Aging and Identity* 6 (2): 93–104.

McPherson, M., L. Smith-Lovin, and J. Cook (2001). "Birds of a Feather: Homophily in Social Networks." *Annual Review of Sociology* 27 (1): 415–44.

Melo, D., and D. Stockemer (2014). "Age and political participation in Germany, France and the UK: A comparative analysis." *Comparative European Politics* 12 (1): 33–53.

Mendelberg, T., C. F. Karpowitz, and J. B. Oliphant (2014). "Gender inequality in deliberation: Unpacking the black box of interaction." *Perspectives on Politics* 12 (1): 18–44.

Meserve, S. A., D. Pemstein, and W. T. Bernhard (2009). "Political Ambition and Legislative Behavior in the European Parliament." *Journal of Politics* 71: 1015–32.

Mills, G., J. Herbst, O. Obasanjo, and D. Davis (2017). *Making Africa Work: A Handbook*. London: Hurst Publishers.

Milner, H. (2010). *The Internet Generation: Engaged Citizens or Political Dropouts*. Medford, MA: Tufts University Press.

Mindich, D. T. Z. (2005). *Tuned Out: Why Americans Under 40 Don't Follow the News*. New York: Oxford University Press.

Morgan, D. L. (1988). "Age differences in social network participation." *Journal of Gerontology* 43 (4): 129–37.

Morone, J. A., and T. R. Marmor (1981). "Representing Consumer Institutions: The Case of American Health Planning." *Ethics* 91: 431–50.

Munger, K. (2021). "Boomer Ballast and the inevitability of intergenerational conflict." https://kevinmunger.substack.com/p/boomer-ballast

Murray, R. (2008). "The Power of Sex and Incumbency: A Longitudinal Study of Electoral Performance in France." *Party Politics* 14 (5): 539–54.

Murray, R. (2014). "Quotas for men: Reframing gender quotas as a means of improving representation for all." *American Political Science Review* 108 (3): 520–32.

Mycock, A., and J. Tonge (2012). "The Party Politics of Youth Citizenship and Democratic Engagement." *Parliamentary Affairs* 65: 138–61.

Narud, H. M., and H. Valen (2000). "Does social background matter?" In P. Esaiasson and K. Heidar (eds.), *Beyond Westminster and Congress*, 83–106. Columbus: Ohio State University Press.

Nemoto, K., E. Krauss, and R. Pekkanen (2008). "Policy Dissension and Party Discipline: The July 2005 Vote on Postal Privatization in Japan." *British Journal of Political Science* 38 (4): 499–525.

Nevens, K. (2012). "The Youth are Revolting." *Harvard International Review* 34 (2): 44–47.

New York Magazine (2018). "12 Young People on Why They Probably Won't Vote."

http://nymag.com/intelligencer/2018/10/12-young-people-on-why-they-probab
ly-wont-vote.html

New York Times (2019). "Students Across the World Are Protesting on Friday. Why?"
March 14. https://www.nytimes.com/2019/03/14/world/europe/climate-action-st
rikes-youth.html

Norris, P. (1999). "Petroleum patriarchy? A response to Ross." *Politics & Gender* 5 (4):
553–60.

Norris, P. (2002). *Democratic Phoenix: Reinventing Political Activism.* New York:
Cambridge University Press.

Norris, P. (2006). "The impact of electoral reform on women's representation." *Acta
Política* 41 (2): 197–213.

Norris, P., and J. Lovenduski (1993). "'If Only More Candidates Came Forward':
Supply-Side Explanations of Candidate Selection in Britain." *British Journal of
Political Science* 23: 373–408.

Norris, P., and J. Lovenduski (1995). *Political Recruitment: Gender, Race and Class in
the British Parliament.* Cambridge: Cambridge University Press.

Norris, P., and M. Franklin (1997). "Social Representation." *European Journal of Political Research* 32 (2): 185–210.

O'Neill, B. (2007). *Indifferent or Just Different? The Political and Civic Engagement of
Young People in Canada.* Ottawa: Canadian Policy Research Network.

Ono, Y. (2012). "Portfolio allocation as leadership strategy: Intraparty bargaining in
Japan." *American Journal of Political Science* 56 (3): 553–67.

Ono, Y. (2015). "Personal Attributes of Legislators and Parliamentary Behavior: An
Analysis of Parliamentary Activities among Japanese Legislators." *Japanese Journal of Political Science* 16 (1): 68–95.

Palmer, B., and S. Dennis (2001). "The political class ceiling." *Women & Politics* 23
(1–2): 59–78.

Paxton, P., M. M. Hughes, and M. A. Painter (2010). "Growth in Women's Political
Representation: A Longitudinal Exploration of Democracy, Electoral System and
Gender Quotas." *European Journal of Political Research* 49 (1): 25–52.

Paxton, P., and S. Kunovich (2003). "Women's political representation: The importance of ideology." *Social Forces* 82 (1): 87–113.

Pedersen, K., L. Bille, R. Buch, J. Elklit, B. Hansen, and H. J. Nielsen (2004). "Sleeping
or Active Partners? Danish Party Members at the Turn of the Millennium." *Party
Politics* 10: 367–84.

Peek, M. K., and N. Lin (1999). "Age differences in the effects of network composition
on psychological distress." *Social Science & Medicine* 49 (5): 621–36.

Pérez-Nievas, S., J. Rama-Caamaño, and C. Fernández-Esquer (2018). "New Wine
in Old Bottles? The Selection of Electoral Candidates in General Elections in
Podemos." In G. Cordero and X. Coller (eds.), *Democratizing Candidate Selection: New Methods, Old Receipts?, 123–46.* Basingstoke: Palgrave Macmillan.

Pfanzelt, H., and D. C. Spies (2019). "The Gender Gap in Youth Political Participation:
Evidence from Germany." *Political Research Quarterly* 72 (1): 34–48.

Phillips, A. (1995). *The Politics of Presence.* New York: Oxford University Press.

Phillips, A. (1998). "Democracy and representation: Or, why should it matter who our representatives are?" In A. Philips (ed.), *Feminism and politics*, 224–40. Oxford: Oxford University Press.

Phillips, D., J. Curtice, M. Phillips, and J. Perry (eds.) (2018). *British Social Attitudes: The 35th Report*. London: The National Centre for Social Research.

Pitkin, H. (1972). *The Concept of Representation*. Berkeley: University of California Press.

Pollack, H. (2017). "We have a political problem no one wants to talk about: Very old politicians." *Vox*, August 7. https://www.vox.com/the-big-idea/2017/8/7/161051 20/politicians-elderly-death-disability-mccain-supreme-court

Pomante, M. J., and S. Schraufnagel (2015). "Candidate age and youth voter turnout." *American Politics Research* 43 (3): 479–503.

Pontes A., M. Henn, and M. D. Griffiths (2018). "Towards a Conceptualization of Young People's Political Engagement: A Qualitative Focus Group Study." *Societies* 8: 1–17.

Praino, R., and D. Stockemer (2012). "Tempus Fugit, Incumbency Stays: Measuring the Incumbency Advantage in the U.S. Senate." *Congress & the Presidency* 39 (2): 160–76.

Prainsack, I. E., and A. Vodanović (2013). "Vital for Democracy, but Do They Realise It? Europe's Youth and the 2014 Elections." *European View* 12 (1): 85–94.

Prihatini, E. (2019). "Women who win in Indonesia: The impact of age, experience, and list position." *Women's Studies International Forum* 72 (1): 40–46.

Pruitt, L. (2017). "Youth, politics, and participation in a changing world." *Journal of Sociology* 53 (2): 507–13.

Pruysers, S., and J. Blais (2018). "A little encouragement goes a (not so) long way: An experiment to increase political ambition." *Journal of Women, Politics & Policy* 39 (3): 384–95.

Rainsford, E. (2017). "Exploring youth political activism in the United Kingdom: What makes young people politically active in different organisations?" *British Journal of Politics and International Relations* 19 (4): 790–806.

Rainsford, E. (2018). "UK Political Parties' Youth Factions: A Glance at the Future of Political Parties." *Parliamentary Affairs* 71: 783–803.

Reiser, M. (2014). "The universe of group representation in Germany: Analysing formal and informal party rules and quotas in the process of candidate selection." *International Political Science Review* 35 (1): 55–66.

Republic of the Philippines (1987). "The 1987 constitution of the republic of the Philippines—article VI." Official Gazette. https://www.officialgazette.gov.ph/const itutions/the-1987-constitution-of-the-republic-of-the-philippines/the-1987-cons titution-of-the-republic-of-the-philippines-article-vi/

Reynolds, A. (2011). *Designing Democracy in a Dangerous World*. New York: Oxford University Press.

Rögler, G. (1962). "Die Lex Villia Annalis." *Klio* 40, JG: 76.

Rose, R. (1987). *Ministers and ministries: A functional analysis*. Oxford: Clarendon Press.

Ruedin, D. (2012). "The representation of women in national parliaments: A cross-national comparison." *European Sociological Review* 28 (1): 96–109.

Russell, A. (2005). "Political Parties as Vehicles of Political Engagement." *Parliamentary Affairs* 58: 555–69.

Saglie, J., G. Ødegård, and J. Aars (2015). "Rekruttering av unge folkevalgte." *Tidsskrift for samfunnsforskning* 56 (3): 259–88.

Sanbonmatsu, K. (2002). "Political Parties and the Recruitment of Women to State Legislatures." *Journal of Politics* 64 (3): 791–809.

Sanbonmatsu, K. (2020). "Women's Underrepresentation in the US Congress." *Daedalus* 149 (1): 40–55.

Scarrow, S. E., and B. Gezgor (2010). "Declining Memberships, Changing Members? European Political Party Members in a New Era." *Party Politics* 16 (6): 823–43.

SCB (2019). "Drygt var femte folkvald hoppade av från kommunfullmäktige." https://www.scb.se/hitta-statistik/statistik-efter-amne/demokrati/allmanna-val/allmanna -val-nominerade-och-valda/pong/statistiknyhet/allmanna-val-nominerade-och -valda-avhopp-2014-2018/

SCB (2020). "Kvinnor, unga och utrikes födda underrepresenterade på tunga poster i landets kommuner." https://www.scb.se/hitta-statistik/statistik-efter-amne/demo krati/amnesovergripande-statistik/undersokning-av-fortroendevalda-i-kommun er-och-regioner/pong/statistiknyhet/undersokningen-om-fortroendevalda-i-kom muner-och-regioner-2019/

Scharpf, F. (1999). *Governing in Europe: Effective and democratic?* Oxford: Oxford University Press.

Schwindt-Bayer, L. (2005). "The incumbency disadvantage and women's election to legislative office." *Electoral Studies* 24 (2): 227–44.

Scott, D., M. Vawda, S. Swartz, and A. Bhana (2011). *Punching below their weight: Young South Africans' voting patterns.* Pretoria: Human Sciences Research Council.

Seery, J. (2011). *Too Young to Run? A Proposal for an Age Amendment to the U.S. Constitution.* University Park: Penn State University Press.

Sevi, S. (2021). "Do Young Voters Vote for Young Leaders?" *Electoral Studies* 69: 1–8.

Seyd, P., and P. Whiteley (2004). "British Party Members: An Overview." *Party Politics* 10: 355–66.

Shah, M., M. Cheng, and R. Fitzgerald (2017). "Closing the loop on student feedback: The case of Australian and Scottish universities." *Higher Education* 74 (1): 115–29.

Shames, S. (2017). *Out of the Running: Why Millennials Reject Political Careers and Why It Matters.* New York: New York University Press.

Shen, Y. A., and Y. Shoda (2021). "How Candidates' Age and Gender Predict Voter Preference in a Hypothetical Election." *Psychological Science* 32 (6): 934–43.

Siaroff, A. (2000). "Women's representation in legislatures and cabinets in industrial democracies." *International Political Science Review* 21 (2): 197–215.

Sloam, J. (2012). "New voice, less equal: The civic and political engagement of young people in the United States and Europe." *Comparative Political Studies* 47 (5): 663–88.

Sloam, J. (2013). "The 'Outraged young': How young Europeans are reshaping the political landscape." *Political Insight* 4 (1): 4–7.

Sloam, J. (2016). "Young voters: Most are for remaining in the EU, yet many will not

vote." https://blogs.lse.ac.uk/brexit/2016/04/18/the-generation-gap-how-young
-voters-view-the-uks-referendum/

Sloam, J., and M. Henn (2019). *Youthquake 2017: The Rise of Young Cosmopolitans in Britain*. Cham: Palgrave Macmillan.

Sorensen, R. J. (2013). "Does aging affect preferences for welfare spending? A study of peoples' spending preferences in 22 countries, 1985–2006." *European Journal of Political Economy* 29: 259–71.

Sota, K. (2018). "The Demographic Issue and Silver Democracy." In Y. Funabashi (ed.), *Japan's Population Implosion*, 131–53. Basingstoke: Palgrave Macmillan.

Soule, S. (2001). "Will they engage? Political knowledge, participation and attitudes of generations X and Y." Prepared for the 2001 German and American Conference "Active Participation or a Retreat to Privacy." https://www.civiced.org/papers/res earch_engage.pdf

Southwell, P. (2014). "How to become a deputee—Lean to the left: Party differences and gender parity in the 2012 National Assembly Elections." *French Politics* 12 (4): 348–56.

Stockemer, D. (2015). "Women's descriptive representation in developed and developing countries." *International Political Science Review* 36 (4): 393–408.

Stockemer, D., and A. Sundström (2018). "Age representation in parliaments: Can institutions pave way for the young?" *European Political Science Review* 10 (3): 467–90.

Stockemer, D., and A. Sundström (2019a). "Youth representation in the European Parliament: Insights from interviews with young Members of the European Parliament (MEPs)." *Intergenerational Justice Review* 5 (1): 4–8.

Stockemer, D., and A. Sundström (2019b). "Do young female candidates face double barriers or an outgroup advantage? The case of the European Parliament." *European Journal of Political Research* 58 (1): 373–84.

Stockemer, D., and A. Sundström (2019c). "Young deputies in the European Parliament: A starkly underrepresented age group." *Acta Politica* 54 (1): 124–44.

Stockemer, D., and A. Sundström (2019d). "Women's representation across different generations. A longitudinal analysis of the European Parliament." *JCMS: Journal of Common Market Studies* 57 (4): 823–37.

Stockemer, D., and A. Sundström (2019e). "Corruption and women in cabinets: Informal barriers to recruitment in the executive." *Governance* 32 (1): 83–102.

Stockemer, D., and F. Rocher. (2017). "Age, political knowledge and electoral turnout: A case study of Canada." *Commonwealth & Comparative Politics* 55 (1): 41–62.

Stolle, D., and C. Cruz (2005). *Youth Civic Engagement in Canada: Implications for Public Policy*. Social Capital in Action: Thematic Policy Studies. Ottawa: Policy Research Inititative.

Sundström, A., and D. Stockemer (2021). "Conceptualizing, measuring and explaining youths' relative absence in legislatures." *PS: Political Science & Politics* 54 (2): 195–201.

Sundström, A., and L. Wängnerud (2016). "Corruption as an obstacle to women's political representation: Evidence from local councils in 18 European countries." *Party Politics* 22 (3): 354–69.

Thebault, R. (2019). "'OK, boomer': 25-year-old lawmaker shuts down heckler during climate change speech." *Washington Post*, November 6. https://www.washingtonpost.com/climate-environment/2019/11/05/ok-boomer-year-old-lawmaker-shuts-down-heckler-during-climate-change-speech/

Thijssen, P., J. Siongers, J. Van Laer, J, Haers, and S. Mels (2016). *Political Engagement of the Young in Europe: Youth in the crucible*. London: Routledge.

Townshend, J. R. (2017). "Lex Villia Annalis, 180 BCE." Oxford Classical Dictionary.

Trantidis, A. (2016). "Is Age a Case for Electoral Quotas? A Benchmark for Affirmative Action in Politics." *Representation* 52 (2–3): 149–61.

Tremblay, M., and D. Stockemer (2013). "Women's ministerial careers in cabinet, 1921–2010: A look at socio-demographic traits and career experiences." *Canadian Public Administration* 56 (4): 523–41.

Tremmel, J., A. Mason, P. Haakenstad, and G. I. Dimitrijoski (2015). *Youth quotas and other efficient forms of youth participation in ageing societies*. Berlin: Springer Verlaag.

Tripp, A. M., and A. Kang (2008). "The global impact of quotas: On the fast track to increased female legislative representation." *Comparative Political Studies* 41 (3): 338–61.

Turkie, A. (2010). "More than crumbs from the table: A critique of youth parliaments as models of representation for marginalised young people." In B. Percy-Smith and N. Thomas (eds.), *A handbook of children and young people's participation: Perspectives from theory and practice*, 262–69. London: Routledge.

Ulbig, S. G., and T. Waggener (2011). "Getting registered and getting to the polls: The impact of voter registration strategy and information provision on turnout of college students." *PS: Political Science & Politics* 44: 544–51.

UNDP (2013). *Enhancing youth political participation throughout the electoral process*. New York: United Nations Development Programme.

UNICEF (2018). "Child marriage in West and Central Africa at a glance." https://www.unicef.org/wca/media/2596/file

United Nations (2016a). "World Youth Report." https://www.un.org/development/desa/youth/world-youth-report.html

United Nations (2016b). "Launching global campaign promoting right of young people to run for public office." https://www.un.org/youthenvoy/2016/11/launching-global-campaign-promoting-rights-young-people-run-public-office/

United Nations (2019). "Per capita GDP at current prices—US dollars." http://data.un.org/Data.aspx?q=GDP+per+capita&d=SNAAMA&f=grID%3a101%3bcurrID%3aUSD%3bpcFlag%3a1

UN Women (2019). "Facts and figures: Leadership and political participation." https://www.unwomen.org/en/what-we-do/leadership-and-political-participation/facts-and-figures

Urdal, H. (2006). "A clash of generations? Youth bulges and political violence." *International Studies Quarterly* 50: 607–29.

Van Gyampo, R. E. (2015). "Youth in Parliament and Youth Representation in Ghana." *Journal of Asian and African Studies* 50 (1): 69–82.

Van Kessel, I. (2000). *'Beyond our wildest dreams': The United Democratic Front and the transformation of South Africa.* Charlottesville: University Press of Virginia.

Van Parijs, P. (1998). "The Disenfranchisement of the Elderly, and Other Attempts to Secure Intergenerational Justice." *Philosophy and Public Affairs* 27 (4): 292–333.

Verba, S., K. L. Schlozman, and H. E. Brady (1995). *Voice and equality: Civic volunteerism in American politics.* Cambridge, MA: Harvard University Press.

Volkens, A., P. Lehmann, T. Matthieß, N. Merz, S. Regel, and B. Weßels (2017). "The Manifesto Data Collection." Manifesto Project (MRG/CMP/MARPOR). Version 2017b. Berlin: Wissenschaftszentrum Berlin für Sozialforschung (WZB). https://doi.org/10.25522/manifesto.mpds.2017b

Wagner, M., D. Johann, and S. Kritzinger (2014). "Voting at 16: Turnout and the quality of vote choice." *Electoral Studies* 31 (2): 372–83.

Wattenberg, M. P. (2015). *Is voting for young people?* London: Routledge.

Weber, L., A. Loumakis, and J. Bergman (2003). "Who Participates and Why? An Analysis of Citizens on the Internet and the Mass Public." *Social Science Computer Review* 21 (1): 26–42.

Weber, R. (2020). "Why do young people join parties? The influence of individual resources on motivation." *Party Politics* 26: 496–509.

Weeks, A. C., and L. Baldez (2015). "Quotas and Qualifications: The Impact of Gender Quota Laws on the Qualifications of Legislators in the Italian Parliament." *European Political Science Review* 7 (1): 119–44.

Weiffen, B. (2004). "The Cultural-Economic Syndrome: Impediments to Democracy in the Middle East." *Comparative Sociology* 3 (3): 353–75.

Weisberg, H. (1987). "Cabinet transfers and departmental prestige: Someone old, someone new, someone borrowed." *American Politics Quarterly* 15 (2): 238–53.

White, H. (1980). "A heteroscedasticity-consistent covariance matrix estimator and a direct test for heteroscedasticty." *Econometrica* 48 (4): 817–38.

Women Deliver. (2017). "How one young leader is getting more young people to run for political office." https://womendeliver.org/2017/one-young-leader-getting-young-people-run-political-office/

Wood, D. M., and G. Young (1997). "Comparing constituency activity by junior legislators in Great Britain and Ireland." *Legislative Studies Quarterly* 22 (3): 217–32.

Worland, J. (2019). "Donald Trump Called Climate Change a Hoax. Now He's Awkwardly Boasting About Fighting It." *Time*, July 8. https://time.com/5622374/donald-trump-climate-change-hoax-event/

World Bank (2019). "Worldwide Governance Indicators." https://info.worldbank.org/governance/wgi/

World Economic Forum (2016). "13 quotes on women and work." https://www.weforum.org/agenda/2016/03/quotes-on-women-at-work/

World Economic Forum (2020). "COVID-19: Young workers in the U.S. are likely to be hit the hardest." https://www.weforum.org/agenda/2020/04/young-workers-covid19-economics-united-states-service-industry-coronavirus

Worldometers (2019). "World Demographics." https://www.worldometers.info/demographics/world-demographics/

Young, I. M. (1989). "Polity and group difference: A critique of the ideal of universal citizenship." *Ethics* 99 (2): 250–74.

Young, I. M. (1997). "Deferring group representation." In I. Shapiro and W. Kymlicka (eds.), *Ethnicity and group rights*, 349–76. Nomos XXXIX. New York: New York University Press.

Index

Page numbers in *italics* denote tables.